Food 2000

Global Policies for Sustainable Agriculture

*A Report of the Advisory Panel on
Food Security, Agriculture, Forestry
and Environment
to the
World Commission on
Environment and Development*

Zed Books Ltd
London and New Jersey

Food 2000: Global Policies for Sustainable Agriculture was first published on behalf of the World Commission on Environment and Development, Palais Wilson, 52 rue des Paquis, CH-1201, Geneva, Switzerland, by Zed Books Ltd., 57 Caledonian Road, London N1 9BU, UK, and 171 First Avenue, Atlantic Highlands, New Jersey 07716, USA, in 1987.

Cover designed by Adrian Yeeles/Artworkers.
Diagrams drawn by Henry Iles.
Typeset by Grassroots Typeset, London.
Printed and bound in the United Kingdom by
Cox & Wyman Ltd., Reading.

British Library Cataloguing in Publication Data

Food 2000 : global policies for sustainable agriculture:
    a report for the World Commission on Environment and
    Development.
    1. Agricultural ecology
    I. World Commission on Environment and Development
    630   S589.7

    ISBN 0-86232-708-3
    ISBN 0-86232-709-1 Pbk

Contents

Foreword   ix

1. **The Challenge**   1
   Sustainable Livelihood Security   3
   The Food Balance   5

2. **Achievements and Crises**   9
   Sub-Saharan Africa   13
   North Africa and West Asia   15
   South and East Asia   16
   Latin America and the Caribbean   19
   Eastern Europe and the USSR   22
   North America, Western Europe, Australasia   23

3. **Transforming Crisis Into Opportunity**   26
   Increasing Yields and Productivity   27
   Land Reform   27
   Development of Human Resources   30
   Energy   34
   Fertilizers, Pesticides, Integrated
     Pest Management   37
   Urban Agriculture   45
   Preserving and Enhancing the Quality
     of the Existing Resource Base   47

       Deforestation   47
         Some Causes Of Deforestation   47
         The Effects Of Deforestation   54
         Forest Policy, Land Classification
           and Forest Management   58

Water And Food Security 60
Irrigation 60
Integrated Water Management 63
Fisheries: Aquaculture 64

Restoring the Land 67
Desertification 67
The Plan of Action to
  Combat Desertification 72
Population 74
Reorienting Agricultural Policy 79
 Global Thinking, National and
  Regional Action 79
 Towards New Agricultural Systems 84
 Financing the Transition to Sustainable
  Agriculture and Food Security 94
 National and International Institutional
  Arrangements 96

**4. Summary of Major Conclusions and
Recommendations** 99

Footnotes 121

Selected Bibliography 123

Annex
Interim Recommendations to WCED on the Food
 and Ecological Crisis in Africa 127

Tables
Table 1 Cereal Production and Population
  Growth 1970-82 7
Table 2 Yields in North-East Brazil in 1981 10
Table 3 Total Land Area and Arable Land
  by Continent 11
Table 4 World Grain Production and Fer-
  tilizer Use 1934-38 to 1979-81 12
Table 5 Growth of Per Capita Food Pro-
  duction between 1973-74 and
  1983-84 in Latin America and the
  Caribbean 20

Table 6   The Changing Pattern of World
           Grain Trade,1950-83   24
Table 7   The Potential (around 1970) for
           Land Reform   30
Table 8   Human Numbers Affected by
           Desertification   73
Table 9   African Population Projections,
           1980-2100   76
Table 10   Population Growth Rates by
           Region, 1950-85   78

Figures

Figure 1   Trends in paddy yield and paddy
           area per capita, South and South-
           East Asia, 1955-84   17
Figure 2   world fertilizer use and grain area
           per person, 1950-83   38
Figure 3   Regional trends of desertification
           within land-use categories and
           major natural resources   68
Figure 4   Rural population affected by
           moderate or severe desertification
           respectively in the major regions
           and subregions of the drylands and
           the main types of land use   70

**List of Members of the Advisory Panel
on Food Security, Agriculture, Forestry and Environment***

Chairman:	Mr. M.S. Swaminathan (India), Director-General of the International Rice Research Institute;
	President of the International Union for Conservation of Nature and Natural Resources
Members:	1. Mr. Nyle Brady (USA) Senior Assistant Administrator, USAID
	2. Mr. Robert Chambers (UK) Rural Development Specialist, IDS, Sussex
	3. Mrs. K. Chowdhry, (India) Chairperson, National Wastelands Development Board, Government of India
	4. Mr. Gilberto Gallopin (Argentina) Director, Department of Natural Resources and Energy, Bariloche Foundation
	5. Mr. Joe Hulse (Canada) Vice President, International Development Research Centre
	6. Mr. Kenneth King (Guyana) Director of Technical Advisory Division UNDP Headquarters
	7. Mrs. V. Malima (Tanzania) Director of Agricultural Research, Ministry of Agriculture
	8. Mr. Samir Radwan (Egypt) Senior Economist Rural Employment Policies Branch International Labour Office
	9. Mr. Lu Liang Shu (China) President of the Chinese Academy of Agricultural Sciences
Special Advisor:	Mr. E.S. Ayensu (Ghana), President,

Secretariat:	E.S. Ayensu Associates Science, Technology and Economic Consultants
	Ms. Shimwaayi Muntemba (Zambia), Coordinator
	Ms. Teresa Harmand (Britain), Secretary
	Ms. Evelyn T. Salvador, (Philippines) Secretary

* Panel Members have supported the work of the Commission in their personal capacity. Views expressed in this document should not be taken as representing their organizations or countries of origin.

Foreword

The World Commission on Environment and Development (WCED) has been asked by the United Nations to develop concrete proposals for reversing the current trends in environmental degradation. In many areas of agriculture and industry, there has been spectacular progress since World War II. Consequently, the world now has over 300 million tons of grain reserves. Yet the number of hungry people is steadily increasing. It is also becoming clear that the pathways adopted so far for improving agricultural and industrial production and productivity are not always based on considerations of the ecological sustainability of the production processes. The Panel on Food Security, Agriculture, Forestry, and Environment set up by the WCED was therefore asked to indicate how humankind can be insulated from hunger on an ecologically sustainable basis. This report contains the suggestions of the Panel on methods of achieving food and nutrition security coupled with the security of the ecological foundations essential for sustained agricultural advance. The Commission will submit its Report and recommendations to the General Assembly in the Autumn of 1987.

The Chairman of WCED, Mrs. Gro Harlem Brundtland, recently stressed the dimensions and urgency of the tasks awaiting us. She said "more people will be added to the planet in the 5000 days remaining between now and the end of the century than existed at the beginning of this century."

She emphasized the need for "new concepts of management that both preserve the essential sovereignity of the individual, his culture, community and nation, and permit the degree of management at the regional and global level needed to guide our common destiny on our one Earth."

In recent years, there have been several global resolutions relevant to sustainable development. Some examples are:

1. The General Assembly of the UN adopted a World Charter for Nature in October 1982.
2. The FAO General Conference adopted a Charter for the Soil in November 1981.
3. The FAO General Conference decided in November 1983 to invite all Member and non-member Nations of FAO to subscribe to an International Undertaking on Plant Genetic Resources, which will ensure the use of genetic variability as a public rather than as a private resource.

From the difficulties we are experiencing in converting all such resolutions into concrete accomplishments, it is clear that we are yet to give attention to achieving a marriage between the world of words and the world of action. For the sustainable use of environmental assets, we need the support of three major groups.

The first is Government. National and, where appropriate, provincial governments will have to develop a package of incentives and disincentives to promote conservation-based development. Governments should also encourage mass media to play a key role in promoting the proper use of national assets and preventing their abuse. Professionals like ecologists, technologists, development administrators and economists comprise the second group. They will have to assist in developing methods of achieving accelerated economic growth without ecological harm. The third and most important group is, of course, the public. It will have to be the principal agent for effective implementation of the eco-development plans. Unfortunately, grassroot level people's organizations which can help to mobilise community endeavour and "people power" in the sustainable use of land and water, in the conservation of flora and fauna and in the prevention of atmospheric and terrestrial pollution do not exist in most developing countries.

The WCED has to provide a blueprint for achieving the goal of a happy global village where the short- and long-term goals of development are in harmony. This goal will remain a distant dream so long as we persist with unidimensional thinking and implementation structures, both in Government and in private enterprise, which are inadequate to meet the challenge of the multidimensional and multifaceted problems we face in making development ecologically sustainable. The Panel has therefore proposed a Seven-Point Action Plan for achieving sustainable food and nutrition security.

Obviously, any Panel examining problems in their global dimensions can only offer macro-solutions for these problems. The Seven-Point Action Plan proposed by us, to be really meaningful, will have to be analysed and converted into appropriate local-level action plans starting with the village as the primary unit of development. The Members of the Panel hope that this report will be of help in promoting a symphonic agricultural system where appropriate attention is paid to every link in the chain beginning with production and ending with consumption. This alone can help us to produce more and more food from less and less land in the decades and centuries ahead.

On behalf of the Panel Members, I wish to express our sincere gratitude to Mrs. Brundtland and the Commissioners of WCED for asking us to undertake this important task. To Mr. Jim MacNeill, Secretary-General of WCED, we owe a deep sense of gratitude for all the help he and the other officers and consultants of the Commission gave us. In particular, thanks to Dr. Shimwaayi Muntemba whose untiring efforts and total dedication to the cause of achieving freedom from hunger on a sustainable basis were of immense help to us. Thanks are also due to Mrs. Teresa Harmand for her competent and dedicated secretarial help. Finally, I wish to thank my fellow members on the Panel for their cooperation and for their inspiring and constructive contributions to the work of the Panel. I would like again to stress that the Panel Members have served in their individual capacity and the views expressed in the report should not be construed in any way as the views of the organizations to which they belong.

M.S. Swaminathan
Chairman
Advisory Panel on
Food Security

1. The Challenge

We live in a world of cruel paradox. Nearly one-fifth of our people live in absolute poverty, in conditions of unacceptable deprivation, squalor and misery. Struggle though they do, they lack entitlements and therefore cannot produce or purchase the food and basic goods they need. They are caught in a poverty trap from which they cannot escape and suffer a hunger they cannot satisfy. Every year, 13 to 18 million people die from hunger and hunger-related diseases. Of these, about 15 million are small children, (18 children under five years of age die every minute). Over 500 million people are chronically hungry.[1]

At the same time, in our same world, mountains of food pile up in the industrialized market economies as well as in some developing countries. The mountains of surpluses are a result of interrelated and ecologically unsound agricultural, economic, trade and aid policies. Excessive subsidies to small pressure groups of farmers are by far the most important factor contributing to such surpluses. The surpluses cause problems not only to the countries that produce and store them but to countries in other regions. In the producing countries, they are threatening the ecological base, particularly the fertility of the soils, the vegetation and the water. This threat to the viability of agro-ecosystems and to public finances has been a source of concern for some time in the affected industrialized countries. Their adverse impact on the development of sustainable agriculture and associated livelihoods in many developing countries has, as yet, hardly registered. The distribution of such subsidized surpluses, either on commercial or concessional terms, depresses prices, competes unfairly with producers in developing countries who need to export to earn foreign exchange, reduces incentives for local food production, destroys the livelihoods of the poor, and drives countries and rural people within them deeper into debt and deprivation.

The processes at work are triply unsustainable. First, high yields in rich countries are based on heavy doses of fertilizer and pesticides and high inputs of non-renewable energy, causing pollution and loss of fertility. Second, rich-country and urban demands for timber, beef, fodder and other products destroy forests and soil fertility in developing countries. Third, within developing countries, urban interests depress prices for rural products. At the same time, local elites acquire rural property, forcing rising numbers of rural dwellers into marginal areas and activities where, in order to survive, they are driven to damage the environment. The processes are complex and varied, but the broad lines are clear. The rural poor and weak are at the end of causal chains which start with the greed of the rich and powerful, both at home and abroad, and with forces that appropriate, damage and destroy the resources on which they depend.

Conventional analysis of questions of environment and development follows a logic which also places the poor at the end of the line, as a residual. In much environmental thinking, conservation of resources is the prime aim, and poor people are seen as a problem to be managed, especially by limiting their access to natural resources. In much developmental thinking, production of food and other commodities is the prime aim, and the poor are supposed to benefit through a "trickle down" process and from the fact that food has been produced and is available on the market. But neither of these approaches tackles, let alone starts with, the problem of the poor themselves, their livelihoods, resources and entitlements. Consequently, in our view, both environmental thinking and developmental thinking on these lines are doomed to failure in their own terms: conservation of resources is undermined by the greed of some of the rich and the desperation of the poor; commodity production cannot be sustained while the ecological base degrades. Neither analytical approach gets to the roots of the problem, or finds a solution, and the world as a human life-support system remains set on a disaster course. A new analysis is needed.

Sustainable Livelihood Security

This new analysis starts with the poor in the cause and effect linkage, where they are, what they have. That their well-being is a moral imperative is not in dispute. But in our view, the practical imperatives for putting poor people first are also overwhelming. These have been inadequately recognized and are fundamental for any long-term strategy. Were the moral and practical imperatives in conflict, there would be grounds for serious debate, and many would still put the poor first. But they are not in conflict. They are mutually supporting. The integrating concept, central to this report, is sustainable livelihood security.

Livelihood is defined as adequate stocks and flows of food and cash to meet basic needs. Security refers to secure ownership of, or access to, resources and income-earning activities, including reserves and assets to offset risk, ease shocks and meet contingencies. Sustainable refers to the maintenance or enhancement of resource productivity on a long-term basis. A household may be enabled to gain sustainable livelihood security in many ways—through ownership of land, livestock, or trees; rights to grazing, fishing, hunting or gathering; through stable employment with adequate remuneration; or through varied repertoires of activities.

Sustainable livelihood security is basic for three practical reasons. First, it is a precondition for a stable human population. The poor lack secure command over resources, expect some of their children to die and rationally have large families as a survival strategy. Their aim is to spread risks by diversifying their sources of food and cash with members in different activities and places, and to have sources of support in their old age. Only when livelihoods are secure, when children survive, and when assets like land, livestock or trees can be passed on to children, does it become rational to limit family size.

Second, secure resources and adequate livelihoods are prerequisites for good husbandry and sustainable management. Insecure tenure prompts quick exploitation with little concern for long-term degradation; secure long-term tenure encourages a long-term view and the investment of labour and funds in

3

resource enhancement. The fact that poor peasants will hold on to their land even in the most distressing situations demonstrates the tenacious ability of the poor to take the long view with resources. But this is only possible with secure rights and when basic needs are met: the dispossessed and the starving cannot concern themselves with sustainability.

Third, sustainable livelihood security reverses destabilizing processes. Secured against a background of rural development, it eases rural to urban migration, thus reducing pressure on urban services and jobs, and weakens the demand for low food prices for the urban poor, thereby allowing incentive prices for rural food production. Increased crop production by the poor, where they are, with resources at their command improves their level of living and generates secondary employment. It reduces the need for food to be produced elsewhere and generally contributes to national economic development.

With its potential for slowing population growth, promoting sustainable resource management and reversing destabilizing trends, sustainable livelihood security presents the key focus for analysis and action.

The challenge of sustainable livelihood security, though widespread, is concentrated in certain developing countries and regions. It is not a challenge simply to raise average productivity and incomes but to raise the productivity and incomes of those poor in resources. The focus should be on their livelihoods and food security, and on reversing the processes of marginalization which threaten and impoverish them. To meet the challenge requires giving higher priority to special programmes of resource redistribution: land, livestock and tree reforms; preference for smallholders, including and especially women, in new land and irrigation development and in technology utilization; reinforcement of the rights of the poor to ownership and use; and the generation of better livelihoods for landless agricultural workers.

The challenge is sharpened by projected population increases in many countries and regions. These mean that in future, larger numbers will have to find their living in rural areas. Fighting the famine of jobs in these areas is allied to fighting the famine of food. Indeed, the nutrition problems in many parts of the developing countries can be improved only by enabling more people to gain livelihoods—adequate, secure and sustainable levels of living—in rural areas. Rapid agricultural development is crucial both to generate the livelihoods necessary to purchase food and to increase its availability. To a large extent, rural development in developing countries implies the generation of land and water-based occupations such as crop and animal husbandry (including wild game), pastoralism, horticulture, fisheries and forestry. In view of this, if countries with untapped agricultural resources respond to rising food demands by increasing food imports, they will in effect be importing unemployment. They will be adding to marginalization and destructive poverty pressures on the resource base.

The Food Balance

The next few decades present a greater challenge to the world's food systems than they may ever face again. The effort needed to increase production in pace with an unprecedented increase in demand, while retaining the essential ecological integrity* of food systems, is colossal both in its magnitude and complexity. Given the obstacles to be overcome, most of them man-made, it can fail more easily than it can succeed.

Looking to the year 2000 and beyond, the global food system must be managed to secure 3 to 4 per cent annual increases in production, which must be sustainable economically, socially and ecologically. If this proves possible over the next 25, 50, 100 years, humankind should be able to support itself indefinitely, given the anticipated slowing of population growth. But can the global food system be so managed?

Population growth is one of the two principal sources of future demand for food products. The human race will add about 1.3 billion members in the remaining years of this century. It will double 40 years later and could reach 11 + billion before stabilizing around the end of the next century.

Rapidly rising incomes in many developing countries will also fuel the demand for food. These may account for 30 to 40 per

---

* ecological integrity refers to the imperatives to conform to principles of sustainable development.

cent of the increase in developing countries and about 10 per cent in developed countries.

Increases in average income will not, however, quell the hunger of those without any income. Almost 20 per cent of the world's population who suffer from starvation and malnutrition do so not because there is a shortage of food, but because they do not possess the income needed to command their share. Indeed, 50 per cent of the world's hungry people live in just five countries, four of which are in Asia where the Green Revolution has taken place and even in one such country where national surpluses have been recorded.

The answer will depend on the capacity of national food systems to respond in the short, medium and long terms. In the short term, a nation's response will depend on its existing endowment of resources and environment, its potential for productivity gains with available technology, its present institutional capability and policy structures, and the available international arrangements to support them. Over the medium and long terms, response will depend on the extent to which a nation has developed and applied policy measures to improve its resource endowment, reduced pressures on its environment and improved its technological and institutional capability.

The problem is not one of global food production being outstripped by population. On the contrary, food grain production has been rising faster than population. The problem has three aspects: where the food is produced, by whom, and who can command it. Table 1 shows cereal production and population growth by region between 1970 and 1982. Globally, there was a per capita increase of 0.5 per cent per annum. There were sharp rises in the industrial market economies (1.6 per cent) and in East Asia and the Pacific (1.8 per cent), and sharp falls in sub-Saharan Africa and some countries in Latin America and the Caribbean. In 1984, per capita production of cereals, roots and tubers, the principle sources of calories, was 860 kg. in the industrial market economies compared to 320 kg. in sub-Saharan Africa (excluding South Africa).[2] The challenge is to slow down on the surpluses of the industrial market economies and to enable the deficit countries, regions and households to produce much more.

Table 1: Cereal Production and Population Growth, 1970-82

	Cereal production	Population	Cereal Production per capita
World	2.3	1.8	0.5
Developing economies	3.0	2.1	0.9
East Africa	0.8	3.0	−2.2
West Africa	1.9	2.7	−0.8
Middle East and North Africa	1.7	2.9	−1.2
East Asia and the Pacific	3.5	1.7	1.8
South Asia	2.7	2.4	0.3
Latin America and Caribbean	3.2	2.4	0.8
Industrial market economies	2.3	0.7	1.6
East European non-market economies	0.6	0.8	−0.2

Source: World Bank study Poverty and Hunger: Issues and Options for Food Security in Developing Counties. Reprinted with permission.

Note: Cereal production includes wheat, rice, maize, rye, sorghum, millet, barley, oats, and mixed grains. All growth rates in all tables have been computed using the least-squares method.

Useful distinctions can be made here between three types of food production systems. The first type is represented by industrial agriculture, which is capital and input intensive and usually large scale. It is dominant in the temperate climates of North America, Europe, Australasia, the East European non-market economies and in their temperate enclaves in many developing countries. Second, there is the Green Revolution agriculture found in uniform, resource-rich, often flat and irrigated conditions, usually in the tropics. It includes 'core' or agricultural heartland areas in developing countries. It is more widely spread in Asia but is also found in parts of Latin America and North Africa. The third type is resource-poor agriculture in developing countries, usually in rainfed and often ecologically diverse, complex and vulnerable conditions with undulating topography. This predominates over most of Sub-Saharan Africa and the hinterlands and more remote areas of Asia and Latin

America. Here, per capita production has been declining and the lack of access to food is most menacing.

Industrial agriculture in the West is, at the moment, producing large surpluses. Green Revolution agriculture has contributed most successfully to increased national food production and surpluses in some countries. At present, however, the benefits of the Green Revolution are enjoyed mainly by the resource-rich farmers. The great new challenge is to broaden its base to include all farmers and pastoralists.

2. Achievements and Crises

Measured solely in terms of global increases in food production and production per capita, the past generation has been one of unprecedented progress in world agriculture. Between 1950 and 1983, while the world population increased from 2.51 billion to 4.66 billion, agricultural production increased by 900 million tons, from 248 kg to 310 kg per capita. However, while this production record is impressive, it hides wide variations in the output performance of different regions and countries. It masks even greater variations in the distribution of food among different socio-economic groups, especially in many developing countries.

A number of recent assessments suggest that, on a global scale, the base of arable lands, forests and waters required to meet the demands ahead is available. The potential for future productivity increases is also thought to be enormous, although the base of healthy, educated and skilled human resources is weak in most of the world.

Before 1950, increases in food output came largely from expanding the area under cultivation. But, with the growing scarcity of accessible land and the advent of cheap chemical fertilizers and pesticides*, this pattern changed dramatically. In 1950, when the world population totalled 2.5 billion, the harvested area of cereals per person was 0.24 ha. By 1983, population growth had reduced the cultivated area per capita to 0.15 ha. At the same time, fertilizer consumption per capita climbed from about 5 kg in 1950 to 25 kg in 1983. The consumption of chemicals to control insects, pests, weeds etc. showed

---

* Including herbicides, insecticides, fungicides

an even sharper increase, rising 32-fold in 35 years.[3]

New varieties of wheat and rice, which have been at the heart of agricultural advances in the developing countries, figured prominently in the growth of output, as did the doubling of the area under irrigation. Many of these varieties, responding well to good management, exhibit a high economic yield (ratio of usable to total plant weight), shorter maturing time (permitting multiple cropping), and/or higher disease resistance. But the effectiveness of the high-yielding varieties depends heavily on the use of market-purchased inputs like mineral fertilizer and pesticides. Industrial agriculture in North America and Europe has depended on chemical fertilizers. Industrial enclaves in developing countries and the Green Revolution areas have also based a substantial portion of output increases on irrigation and fertilizers as much as on the other factors of production mentioned above. FAO estimates that fertilizers accounted for 55 per cent of the increase in yield in developing countries between 1965 and 1976. Table 2 exemplifies the dramatic effect of increased fertilizer dosage in one part of one such country, Brazil.

Table 2: Yields in North-East Brazil in 1981

Crop	Yield without fertilizer	NPK*	Yield increase %
Cotton	507	1,130	123
Rice	1,878	3,111	66
Groundnuts	1,144	2,198	92
Sugar Cane	59,228	87,028	47
Beans	571	1,103	93
Cassava	15,092	26,060	73
Maize	1,528	3,026	98

* NPK—Nitrogen, phosphorous and potassium

Source: I. Szabolcs. *Proceedings of 9th Congress of the International Centre of Fertilizers*. Vol 1. (Budapest, 1984)

Pesticides have also contributed to increased yields. Starting with industrialized countries, pesticides soon found ready markets in developing countries where governments encouraged their use through subsidies. They have contributed significantly to the increased yields in several food and industrial crops obtained in all industrialized and many developing countries, and offer opportunities for conquering more land for agricultural expansion, provided they are applied in environmentally sustainable ways.

Global figures are deceptive, however, masking significant differences between and within regions and countries and among the various social groups having access to land. Table 3 summarizes some of these differences in land. Latin America and sub-Saharan Africa are especially well endowed, although here again aggregate figures mask the high variability of land between the land-abundant and land-short countries and the quality and vulnerability of the unexploited arable lands. The Soviet Union and parts of North America have some significant amounts of frontier land left that is suitable for agriculture; only Asia and Europe are truly land-starved regions.

Table 3: Total Land Area and Arable Land by Continent

Continents	Total land area	Cultivated land	Potential arable land	% of land area cultivated	% of arable land cultivated
	(in millions of hectares)				
Africa	3,010	158	734	5.2	22
Asia (not USSR)	2,740	519	627	18.9	83
Australia & New Zealand	820	32	153	3.9	21
Europe	480	154	174	32.1	88
North America	2,110	239	465	11.3	51
South America	1,750	77	681	4.4	11
USSR	2,240	227	356	10.1	64
Total	*13,150*	*1,406*	*3,190*	*10.7*	*44*

Source: I. Szabolcs. As adapted from the Global 2000 Report to the President of the United States.

11

The response of crops, worldwide, to fertilizer use is now diminishing, as shown in Table 4. During the 1950s, the application of an additional ton of fertilizer produced an additional 11.5 tons of grain. By the 1970s, the ratio had dropped to 5.8 tons. Other inputs bridged the gap and sustained increasing yields. However, as already stated, average figures are deceiving. In this case, they reflect falling marginal productivity in North America and Europe. Most countries in Asia, Africa and Latin America still apply relatively little fertilizer and so still have quite high response ratios.

Table 4: World Grain Production and Fertilizer Use 1934-38 to 1979-81

	World Grain Production*	Increment	World Fertilizer Use	Increment	Incremental Grain/Fertilizer Response Ratio
	——————— (million metric tons) ———————				
1934-38	651		10		
1948-52	710	59	14	4	14.8
1959-61	848	138	26	12	11.5
1969-71	1,165	317	64	38	8.3
1979-81	1,451	286	113	49	5.8

* Annual Average for period

Source: 1934-38 data from Food and Agriculture Organization Production Year-book (Rome: various years): U.S. Department of Agriculture. *World Indices of Agricultural and Food Production*. 1950-82 (unpublished printout. Washington, D.C., 1938):

Food and Agricultural Organization *1977 Annual Fertilizer Review* (Rome, 1978); 1979-81 data from Paul Andrilenas: compiled by World Watch.

It has proved far more difficult to raise world output by a consistent 3 per cent a year in the mid-1980s than it was in the mid-1950s. It may be even more difficult by the mid 1990s. Unless agriculture acquires a much higher priority in developing countries by adopting differential access to inputs (credit, fertilizer, etc.) in favour of resource-poor farmers, and unless agricultural policy acquires an ecological foundation, the crises feared by the turn of the century are inevitable. The changing land/water/forestry/energy/population relationship compounded by the economic crisis weighs heavily on the human prospect. A reorientation of agricultural research and development strategies so as to promote a steady improvement in the productivity, stability, profitability and sustainability of major farming systems is necessary.

Sub-Saharan Africa

Development in many countries of sub-Saharan Africa went into reverse gear during the 1980s. Rates of economic and social advance were outstripped by the most menacing land degradation and highest rates of population growth in the world. The world economic crisis hit the region with special force, undermining its efforts to deliver to its populations the necessary goods and services, including food. Hunger became a chronic part of the landscape and Africa entered both a food crisis and a general economic crisis.

Agriculture in this region is dominated by technologically resource-poor farmers and pastoralists. The soils also are fragile, water scarce and the climate variable. In the 1950s and 1960s, the region was marked by increasing agricultural productivity, including food. But since the beginning of the 1970s average food production per capita has been falling by about 1 per cent per annum and the capacity of the region to feed itself has been and is declining. Inadequate production of staple foods and growing urban tastes for non-traditional foods are creating a growing dependence on imported foods, which the precarious and/or deteriorating economic situation does not easily allow or does so at the expense of satisfying other needs.

At the same time, the region has been experiencing high rates of rural-urban migration. With no urban prospects for employment, many join the throng of the urban poor who are unable to create sufficient incomes to enable them to gain economic access to food.

Deterioration in health and nutrition has become endemic. The most helpless victims are the children, who reflect this deterioration most quickly. The number of severely hungry children has risen 25 per cent in the last decade. Malnutrition may now be so widespread that it will lead to increasing physical and mental impairment over the next decade. Child mortality in all of sub-Saharan Africa was 50 per cent higher than that in other developing countries in the 1950s; now it is almost 100 per cent higher.

The combination of declining per capita output, land and environmental degradation and the rising population growth, against a background of an adverse international economic environment, is setting the stage for a human tragedy of vast proportions. The first acts of this tragedy have already been performed and others will surely follow. Widespread famine, internal strife, war and political instability add to the drama and divert resources essential to improve the African condition. As a result of uneven distribution and inequitable ownership patterns, 40 per cent of the population will face severe land shortages by the year 2000, a proportion that will grow rapidly through the next century since population stabilization will come later in Africa than anywhere else.

A few countries have been able to turn the tide and attain production levels in excess of population growth, for example Tanzania, Rwanda, Ivory Coast and Niger. In a continent beleaguered by conflict and despair, they provide grounds for hope that other countries can do the same.

The potential hidden in the physical and human resources of Africa is in fact enormous and exceeded only by the potential for increased yields and productivity. Less than 25 per cent of the arable land in Africa is cultivated, vast tracts remaining underused, having been acquired by the new urban elites. Use of fertilizer, as of other inputs, is low; only 15.7 per cent of its irrigation potential has been exploited. If the average level of technology was raised to that of the best prevailing in some areas of the continent, gains in yields would be startling.

Development of much of Africa for sustainable agriculture depends on overcoming some basic environmental as well as economic, institutional and political problems. A significant percentage of the 521 million ha. of potentially arable land is unusable because of infestation by the tsetse-fly and other insects. Moreover, as in Latin America, the dominant soils in certain areas are the so-called "acid infertile oxisoils and ultisoils''. Only 19 per cent of the land area is free from inherent fertility limitations, while 44 per cent is drylands. Although West and Central Africa supports luxuriant growth, much of the nutrient supply is tied up in vegetation and ground litter, and most of that is stored in the soil near the surface. When the land is cleared for crop production, the nutrient supply falls and that stored in the soil is readily leached or carried away by run-off from heavy tropical rains. In addition, precipitation is low and erratic over much of the region so that only 56 per cent of the land area is climatically suitable. Clearly, high priority should be given to developing technology which would permit use of such land for agriculture and which would allow multiple cropping patterns.

We believe that Africa's limitations can be overcome through spreading and developing new technologies to all farmers, with the focus on the majority who are small farmers; by exploiting to the full the natural and human resource potential; and by promoting productive but sustainable land-use and farm management patterns. To effect this would require the strengthening of national agricultural systems in order to develop, with the farmers, the necessary locality-specific research and technologies.

North Africa and West Asia

The region suffers from very limited availability of arable land. Only 4.38 per cent of North Africa's land area, for example, is arable and permanent cropland. Desert conditions prevail. This has posed great challenges to the countries in their attempts to attain food self-sufficiency. However, a number of countries recorded increased per capita economic growth in excess of 2 per cent between 1960-70; they were joined by more countries between 1970-79. Given the natural constraints, this caused the region to become the largest food importer among developing regions. In the early 1980s one country ranked among the world's leading recipients of food aid.

The growth achieved in food and imports through production self-sufficiency did not assure food entitlements by all populations. In many countries, food poverty increased. International and regional factors prejudicial to food security worsened the situation, particularly for the poor. Countries suffered from a decline in the terms of trade as prices for their commodities, such as fruit and vegetables, declined; the oil shocks in the 1970s and 1980s have exposed the fragility of an import-based food security. The region has experienced widespread internal migrations. Jobs, and thus the food security of large sections of labour, have been threatened periodically as a result of international crises and heavy debt-servicing burdens on one hand and political tensions on the other.

Some countries, for example Egypt, have long exploited the potential of their water resources. In recent years, significant increases in production have been possible because of controlled irrigation which makes the cultivation of high-yielding varieties feasible. The above constraints have made the irrigation, if it can be maintained in a sustainable way, even more appealing. For other countries, as demonstrated by Israel, Libya, and Saudi Arabia, the constraints have increased the need for, and economic attractiveness of, measures to restore lands lost to desertification. Israel's experience in the control of desertification is particularly valuable. The richer oil exporting countries are investing heavily in irrigated agriculture. Some countries, such as Saudi Arabia, have achieved impressive increases in grain production, almost reaching self-reliance, although this is achieved at high cost due to heavy subsidization policies.

With the human and technological resources available, this region can increase its ability to provide and maintain livelihood security for its people. But this can be achieved only if the land tenure systems are reformed to ensure equitable distribution and productivity.

South and East Asia

This region is today home to more than half the world's people, so agricultural performance in this area is of fundamental importance to global food security. In recent years owing to adoption of new and efficient technologies, many countries in the region, for example China, India, Indonesia, Sri Lanka and Pakistan, have shown a remarkable ability to increase food production,

Figure 1

TRENDS IN PADDY YIELD AND PADDY AREA PER CAPITA
SOUTH AND SOUTHEAST ASIA , 1955 – 1984 .

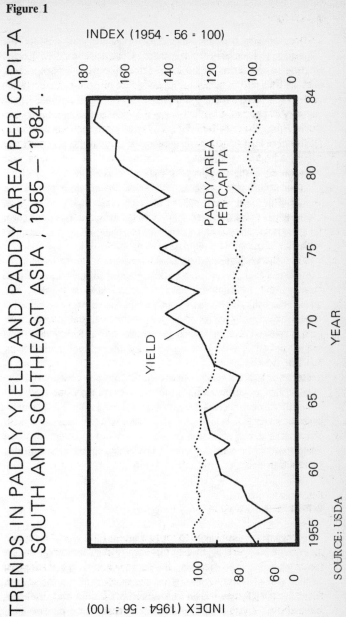

INDEX (1954 - 56 = 100)

YIELD

PADDY AREA
PER CAPITA

YEAR

INDEX (1954 - 56 = 100)

SOURCE: USDA

17

catching up with and keeping ahead of population growth (see Figure 1). However, inequitable social distribution systems continue to deny access to hundreds of millions of people. Over half a billion Asians live in absolute poverty and over 40 per cent of the world's hungry people live in four of the region's countries. The worst affected are the rural and urban poor who own neither land nor livestock and have no other asset. Clearly, entitlements of the poor, especially the landless, must be increased and sustained.

Figures for the last 10 years show food production in East Asia rising about 1 per cent per annum faster than population and in China, for example, at a much faster and higher rate. These results should permit a gradual improvement in nutrition levels, if they can be sustained and broadened and combined with further economic and social progress.

But Asia has little unused land; agricultural land is a shrinking resource as population multiplies and urbanization forces its way into the countryside. Asia's ratio of land to people—0.21 ha per person—is the lowest in the world and falling rapidly. Within the time horizon of this discussion, the situation could be aggravated—seriously so in countries like Bangladesh and Indonesia—by land loss through rises in sea level as the result of climatic change.

Growing land scarcity means that Asian countries will have to seek future increases in output from higher productivity and even greater cropping intensity per unit of arable land, water, forests, energy, labour and time. The FAO estimates that well into the next century, rice production alone must increase by more than 3 per cent per year.[4] This will require a continuous increase in productivity and/or intensity, and it must be done without damaging the potential of the soil—a challenge to policy, people and institutions.

Fortunately, on the production side, fertilizer use is low relative to land and labour and the marginal productivity of increased use is high, providing that adequate supplies of water and high-yielding seeds are available. The prospects for a continuing stream of high-yielding seeds are better in Asia than in Latin America or Africa. The International Rice Research Institute (IRRI) pioneered the development of high-yielding varieties for Asian countries jointly with national research systems. Most Asian countries have strong national research systems that work together with international agricultural research centres in a mutually supportive manner.

The potential for improved water use in Asia is also high but not through the conventional measures of more large dam and irrigation projects. The most accessible of these have already been developed, too often in ways that have gradually undermined the ecological basis of the projects. Siltation, waterlogging and salinization that might have been avoided transfer curative costs to the next generation.

The potential for improved water use rests with better management and co-ordination of existing large and medium-scale irrigation projects and a systematic extension of small projects and of efficiency measures to release water to them. Fortunately, these measures are usually the most cost-effective. The potential provided by groundwater must be explored and exploited. Asia is a continent of small-scale farmers: 75 per cent of them cultivate less than two ha. of land. Moreover, rice production is labour intensive in South-East Asia. For example, an increase of one million tons in rice production may require the active participation of 2 million farming families. Hence, production projects that are not designed to promote the active involvement of millions of small-farmer families will not succeed in their goals.

The intensity of land use will increase the need and the economic attractiveness of measures to reduce further land loss from soil erosion, desertification and salinization, as well as measures to restore land already lost.

Latin America and the Caribbean

On average, Latin America and the Caribbean more than kept pace with population growth during the past decade (the average annual per capita growth rate both of agricultural and food output was 0.6 per cent in the period 1970-80, compared with 0.1 per cent for the period 1960-1970).[5] Although the higher rate of food demand led to increased cereal imports, the total growth of per capita food production for the period 1973-74 to 1983-84 reached 7.7 per cent (Table 5). After 1980, the volume of food imports declined. In some countries—Suriname, Cuba, Brazil, Uruguay, Colombia and Argentina [6]—per capita food production increased more than 10 per cent during the period. In the recent past, the food production sector has been responsive to demand (internal and external) and to the stimuli of government policies.

Table 5: Growth of per capita food production between 1973-74 and 1983-84 in Latin America and the Caribbean

(in percentage over the whole period)

Suriname	+ 51.5
Cuba	+ 28.9
Brazil	+ 23.1
Uruguay	+ 12.7
Colombia	+ 11.3
Argentina	+ 11.1
Chile	+ 9.5
ALL REGION	+ 7.7
Mexico	+ 3.5
Paraguay	+ 1.9
Guatemala	− 0.9
Barbados	− 1.5
Panama	− 1.6
Honduras	− 6.5
Dominican Republic	− 6.9
El Salvador	− 8.9
Haiti	− 11.8
Guyana	− 12.1
Venezuela	− 12.2
Ecuador	− 12.4
Jamaica	− 13.4
Costa Rica	− 15.2
Nicaragua	− 17.0
Bolivia	− 19.4
Peru	− 20.3
Trinidad and Tobago	− 32.6

Source: FAO Production Yearbook, 1984

In 1983-84, per capita food production in 19 of the countries in the region declined. It is important to note that the 7.7 per cent per capita regional expansion of food production was mostly linked to food exports, with almost no impact on the lower-income population. The per capita production of traditional mass-consumption foods over the ten-year period fell sharply. In the last five years, the regional rate of output and agricultural growth has stagnated, and the current financial crisis, reducing the level of investment, has exacerbated the situation. Adjustment policies have reduced domestic demands; high international interest rates and governmental debt servicing have discouraged private and public investments in agriculture; and external demand is diminishing.

According to the FAO estimates [7], the proportion of people with a daily energy intake of less than the critical limit of 1.2 basal metabolic rate (BM) decreased from 13 per cent of the total population in 1970 to 11 per cent in 1980 (but their absolute numbers increased from 36 million to 38 million in the period). The estimated proportion ingesting less than 1.4 BM changed from 19 per cent to 16 per cent (but the actual numbers went up from 53 to 56 million) in the same period. A basic characteristic of the situation is the unequal distribution of food among the different socio-economic groups. The available data invariably show that the poorest sectors of the population have access to less food; their food situation is deteriorating more markedly and more severely than for the average population. Recently, some governments have been taking measures to mitigate the effects of the crisis upon the most vulnerable sectors, ranging from subsidizing food prices to food distribution programmes directly targeted towards the poorest groups.

In contrast with Asia, Latin America possesses both a huge resource and a high productivity potential. South America has the highest proportion of land area that is potentially arable but only 15 per cent of that land is currently cultivated. In Central America and Mexico, just over 25 per cent of the area is suitable for rainfed agriculture; about 50 per cent of its potentially arable lands are under cultivation. Most of the estimated 535 million ha of potentially arable land is in the remote, lightly populated Amazon basin. It has been estimated that perhaps 20 per cent of the lands of the Amazon are suitable for sustainable agriculture, but the knowledge base on which to select these lands is very weak. The policy framework and the technical and institutional capacity to oversee a systematic process of settlement is not in place and will take years to develop, even assuming an underlying political consensus and strong political will.

Neither can be assumed.

Colonization of the Amazon during the last decade has been, in general, ecologically destructive; in many cases land in the Amazon was bought by rich economic sectors of the major cities, who operated as absentee landlords and did not care for the fate of the land. At the same time, following the opening of new roads, landless people migrated anarchically to the area, without having access to agricultural inputs or know-how. To ensure the sustainability of production in this area will require broad social and economic reforms. The Amazonian forests, with their high diversity and ecological productivity, can also represent a huge untapped resource through the use of new technologies, for example biotechnology.

Latin America also has a high productivity potential. Average yields are low compared with developed countries and with what many foresters and farmers in Latin American countries have achieved through improved technology and management practices. With proper socio-economic and agricultural policies and good management, Latin America can absorb a steady increase of improved seed varieties, fertilizers, pesticides, and especially integrated pest management schemes.

Eastern Europe and the USSR

The region as a whole has experienced fluctuating levels of food production over the last three decades due to a high degree of climatic instability and in many cases organizational difficulties. Production increased in some of the countries in the 1950s and 1960s due to expansion of agriculture into virgin lands, and irrigation. In Hungary, for example, co-operative production systems also seem to have contributed.

But the region suffered from disastrous harvests in the 1970s and 1980s. Some Eastern European countries have been recovering from these bad harvests; in 1983 production was believed to have been up by about 4.5 per cent on the previous year. But this still fell short of the peak attained in 1978 and dependence on imports persisted. The picture in some countries still remains bleak unless technological resources and farming skills are marshalled to anticipate and cope with adverse conditions on one hand and to increase and sustain high yields on the other.

While remaining the world's largest wheat producer, the USSR became the world's largest grain importer. Imports of about 40 million tons per year [8] were necessary to meet the demand; the figure is particularly high because of the need for feed grains arising from the nation's heavy intake of animal products. Unlike other importing countries, the USSR requirements have been anticipated in the plans of the major exporters. A significant proportion of its imports is covered by multi-year trading agreements, notably with the United States.

Over the last two to three years, the Soviet Union has stepped up its production, and this is reflected in the decline of world trade in grain. Increased production results from heavy investment in agriculture and greater use of high-yielding seeds. To its capital and technological assets is added some frontier land which the USSR still commands. If agricultural development continues as planned, the import needs of the USSR should go on declining.

The region, however, is greatly threatened by soil and water degradation, in some countries more than in others. It has been reported that cow's milk in parts of Poland, for example, has been contaminated as a result of soil contamination. Acidification, salinization and alkalization are widespread and growing rapidly. The worst menace is posed by ground and surface-water contamination resulting from industrial mismanagement, including over-use of chemicals.

North America, Western Europe and Australasia

Countries in these areas represent the most advanced form of industrial agriculture. They have seen remarkable increases in food production driven by high levels of government intervention, including the richest subsidy structures in the world. Between 1970 and 1982, almost two-thirds of the additional volume of cereals entering world trade came from North America, with the US accounting for more than half the increase. [9] While the European Community remains the world's largest importer of agricultural and food products, principally of tropical fruits and early vegetables, it too generated ever increasing volumes of surpluses for export. However, there are clear warning signs that for most of the countries future increases in production of the same order of magnitude cannot be sustained and should not be contemplated largely because of the ecological costs.

Table 6: The Changing Pattern of World Grain Trade 1950-83*

Region	1950**	1960	1970	1980	1983
North America	+23	+39	+59	+131	+122
Latin America	+ 1	0	+ 4	− 10	− 3
Western Europe	−22	−25	−30	− 16	+ 2
E. Europe/USSR	0	0	0	− 46	− 39
Africa	0	− 2	− 5	− 15	− 20
Asia	− 6	−17	−37	− 63	− 71
Australia/New Zealand	+ 3	+ 6	+12	+ 19	+ 9

Notes: * Plus sign indicates net exports: minus sign, net imports.
** Average for 1948-52

Source: UN FAO. *Production Yearbook* (Rome: various years); US Dept of Agriculture, Foreign Agriculture Circular, (August 1983); compiled by Worldwatch.

Countries such as the US and Australia still have some frontier areas suitable for intensive agricultural production. However, their development poses very high costs and will at best advance slowly. A significant water potential also exists in the regions, but it is dependent upon efficiency measures which, in spite of their cost effectiveness, have so far proved almost impossible to introduce. Other countries have limited unused arable land, much of their prime land having been claimed already for agriculture, urban and industrial spread.

On the other hand, improved land use in North America and Western Europe means withdrawing a vast acreage of marginal land from the production of food grains. The rich subsidies, provided through government intervention programmes, coupled with high export demand, have induced farmers to bring large acreages of marginal land under intensive cultivation.

Some governments have initiated policies that will have long-term impacts on the sustainability of agriculture. For example, the US Government has recently taken steps to modify its structure of subsidies. The Canadian Government has received an alarming report on the economic costs of the environmental effects of its policies and may take similar steps. In 1985, for the first time, the European Community Commission's Green Paper on the Common Agricultural Policy (CAP) raised serious questions about the environmental costs of the CAP as well as their economic costs. Public voice has been added to government concern.

The productivity growth potential of North America and Western Europe is low compared to what it was 10 to 20 years ago and compared to what it is in most developing countries. In North America, the rate of increase in output per ha and in total productivity slowed significantly following the run-up in energy prices in 1973. Fertilizer use per ha in Western Europe is higher than in North America and its marginal productivity is low. There is also a growing concern that over-use of fertilizers in many areas, often encouraged by government intervention programmes, has resulted in significant present and future costs in the form of land degradation and nitrate pollution of surface and ground-waters. In addition, Western Europe (and parts of Eastern Europe) may be forced in the future to retire large acreages condemned by acidification. This could also involve extremely high future costs of rehabilitation.

Taken all together, the picture conveyed is one of further increases in output from North America, Europe and Australasia over the short to medium term, although at a steadily reducing rate. In the long term, the sustainability of the agricultural-resource base for food production may also not be assured, given the rates and extent of soil and water contamination. If this is a correct picture, it will become not only desirable but also necessary for a larger proportion of the anticipated increase in food demand in Asia, Latin America, Africa and the Soviet Union to be met from their own resources.

3. Transforming Crisis Into Opportunity

The potential for sustainable agriculture and livelihood varies greatly between regions and countries. Latin America and Africa have a high potential in both resources and productivity; Asia has a low resource but high productivity potential; North America is comparatively low in both; Western Europe has neither. Therefore tapping the potential of Asia, Africa and Latin America should be one of the priority strategies for global food security.

But the physical resource base for agriculture is deteriorating on almost every continent at varying rates: erosion in North America, soil acidification in Europe, deforestation and desertification in Asia, Africa and Latin America; and pollution and leaching of the water frontier almost everywhere. Within 40 to 70 years, climatic change may begin to deplete the resource base of coastal states dramatically. Strategies to increase production and livelihoods have to start from this premise.

Three strategies are seen as essential to achieve the projected increases in food production: increasing yields and productivity; preserving and enhancing the quality of the resource base; and assisting some countries to restore and rehabilitate lands already lost to production.

In developing countries, the above strategies can be meaningful only if they are associated with a greatly increased access to land and other assets: water, credit and new technology, especially for small farmers, in order to ensure livelihoods for all, particularly the poor.

These measures, while necessary, are by no means sufficient. Countries must also adopt at least three additional directions in global food strategy: reorient economic, trade, energy and other policies in order effectively to integrate environment and development; increase funding for the reorientation of research programmes directed to help resource-poor farmers in particular; and strengthen related institutions and international support measures especially in relation to the debt problem of most developing countries in Africa and Latin America.

Increasing Yields and Productivity

Sustainable increases in yields and productivity are not solely a matter of increasing the use of chemicals, water and energy. Providing a steady stream of new, high-yielding seeds and schemes for integrated pest management are also critical and, tied to that, halting indiscriminate deforestation and the accelerating loss of genetic resources.

Land Reform

In developing countries, food and agriculture need a new deal, an essential part of which is more equitable access to productive assets, including land, livestock and water, as well as all the inputs and services needed to make the land more productive. A prerequisite for this is a broad-based land reform and, through land reform, increased equity and the creation of new rural power structures. Where land reform has occurred, from Eastern Europe to China, from Japan, Korea and Taiwan to India, Pakistan and Cuba, these aims have been largely achieved. The record of post-reform performance is mixed, however, and much has depended on complementing land reform with the institutions and policies that promote production, equity and productive accumulation. The creation of a balanced system of incentives at the individual, sectoral and country level is also crucial to the success of this reform.

The infinite variety, among and within countries in land ownership, land use, farming systems, institutional structures and ecological conditions means that no universal approach to improved access to productive assets is possible. Redistribution of land, however, is basic. Without it, the institutional and policy

27

changes that come about, including those introduced to protect the resource base, may actually worsen distribution, and serve the interests of a minority of large farmers who are better able to obtain the limited supplies of credit and other available services. In thus leaving hundreds of millions without options, the minority would instead ensure the continued violation of ecological imperatives and the collapse of the development process.

FAO has estimated that, given existing patterns of land distribution, the number of smallholders and landless households would increase by about 50 million to nearly 220 million by the year 2000. It points out that together, these groups make up three-quarters of the total number of agricultural households in developing countries.[10] It is questionable whether the required increases in food production can be achieved if these people are excluded from the benefits of improved distribution of inputs and services.

Land reform and the small farm are key instruments for achieving the sustainable increases in yields and productivity needed for future food security. Because food security would reduce the need for food imports, it would also have a favourable impact on a nation's balance of payments and debt, and release capital for other development and release priorities.

The scope for land redistribution is shown in Table 7, from which it is evident that the potential is significant even in densely populated East Asia. The greatest inequality in land distribution is in Latin America where the hacienda can be as large as 20,000 ha., which are often unused or underused, and the minifundia less than one ha. In Africa, political independence seldom altered the colonial pattern of land distribution, which had pushed many peasants into fragile lands. In many countries it actually reinforced and extended it, with politicians and civil servants augmenting the ranks of large landholders and occupying underutilized farms.

Redistribution of land is the most difficult of all social reforms to carry through. Given experience to date, significant progress in this direction may be too much to expect. If this is so, then it is difficult to imagine the needed increases in food production being achieved by the turn of the century. It is even more difficult to imagine the gains achieved being sustained. In some

Table 7: The Potential (around 1970) for Land Reform

	Latin America	Africa	Near East	Far East
Percentage of area currently farmed by smallholders*	3.7	22.4	11.2	21.7
Excess area of large holdings above indicative ceilings as percentage of total area**	65	22	34	12

Notes: * In Latin America a smallholding is less than 10 hectares; in the Near East, less than 5; in Africa and the Far East no more than 2 hectares.

** Indicative ceilings beyond which a farm may be considered "a large landholding" vary from 100 hectares in Latin America to 20 hectares in West Asia and 10 hectares in Africa and East Asia.

Source: FAO: Agriculture: Toward 2000 (Rome, 1981)

countries, projected population increases, superimposed on existing landholding patterns, will result in an incredible increase in poverty-derived pressures on the environment, with accelerated erosion, deforestation and desertification along with continued loss of the genetic resources needed to provide a steady stream of new seed varieties.

A global food strategy guided by realism should pursue a two-track approach: first, to the degree possible, concerted economic, trade and aid policies to induce countries to carry through meaningful land reform and to support the necessary follow-through measures; and second, an increase in the capacity of designated international bodies to anticipate crises and to marshal resources both to respond to crisis and to transform crisis into opportunity, to force through land reform and related measures.

In this regard, multilateral and bilateral aid agencies should extend support to all land and livestock reform measures. Livestock reform is a neglected but extremely important area needing attention, particularly with a view to protecting the pastoral communities of Africa.

Development of Human Resources

In many developing countries, land reform is the basis for agricultural development and enduring food security. Yet it must be acknowledged that, by itself, land is useless. To be rendered productive, it has to be developed, and how this is done will determine the extent of its productivity and usefulness. In this context, we wish to highlight the great importance of human ingenuity as a resource. Human resource development cannot be divorced from issues of ecological rehabilitation and food security. Indeed, it is the key to attaining sustainable development of the biosphere. In addressing the question, we would stress three approaches:

1. to review secondary and university education and training at the country level to assure the necessary supply of scientists;
2. full utilization of the trained personnel and of the available labour in the field; and
3. fair returns to labour.

Formal Education — Scientists: Scientists and engineers are needed to introduce appropriate irrigation systems, to develop suitable technologies for seed production and animal breeding, for sound cropping systems, etc. Some developing regions and countries are reasonably well endowed with well-qualified scientists; others, such as Africa and West Asia, still need to train many more.

But it is not enough to have large numbers of scientists. They have to be qualified to work in specific agro-ecosystems and have the right orientation towards the local people and the areas in which they are to work. This is particularly the case with regard to the hinterlands and to the resource-poor farmers. The right orientation will be reflected in the will to work for, and also to learn from, the traditional farmers who are more conversant with local environments; it would mean developing suitable technologies in situ with them; it would entail living in the areas for as long as necessary.

In developing countries, the curricula found in many schools, colleges and universities, however, are still largely modelled on the Western system, and do not reflect adequately the local ecosystems and socio-economic realities. Many scientists are sent to outside institutions while their own colleges and universities continue to rely on European and American textbooks and external examiners.

Instead of helping produce local scientists, the curricula result in the creation of mismatched people, with the consequence that many qualified nationals have migrated to the outside world in whose institutions they fit better and where they are offered better facilities for their scientific pursuits. That some academic institutions in regions like Africa and Latin America continue to decline while some decision makers have shown a preference and higher respect for expatriate ''experts'' has only added to the outflow of scientists. The few highly qualified scientists who have remained in their own countries have contributed tremendously to agrarian productivity in their respective countries and continue to do so.

In most cases, education does not provide the basic and elementary skills required to cater for the largest sector of the economy, agriculture: skills such as the maintenance of pumps, tractors, threshers, etc. The result has been a mismatch between the products of the education system and the needs of the various productive sectors.

Basic science, biology in particular, needs to be introduced and extended into primary, especially rural, schools. Since a science teacher for every school is an impracticable goal, some alternative methods such as mobile science laboratories and visual aids need to be considered. Equally essential are basic texts which relate to and illustrate local flora and fauna, crops commonly grown and hazards to which they are susceptible, the plant-soil-water relations and animal husbandry from the local perspective.

Producers: Enduring food security rests with farm and fish families and pastoralists. Educational opportunities should be opened up to them. This is especially true of women who make up 60 per cent of the estimated 800 million illiterates in the Developing World. The most that many peasants receive is a primary education. But even this should expose them to modern technology and the behaviour of markets beyond their geographical horizons. With this type of background, a working relationship, with mutual respect, can be developed between producers, natural scientists and economists and in situ extension programmes can become more easily adopted.

Extension workers, "change agents", etc. must be able to visit villages and provide in situ training, thus developing with the farmers themselves technologies suitable to the users and the ecosystems. In addition, peasants are exposed to the successful experiences of others. The concept of field days can be extended to cover visits to other parts of the country and possibly to neighbouring countries.

Women play a critical role in food production: in cultivation, seed selection, storage; in some regions they are the basis for successful afforestation efforts; they provide the main labour on the minifundia in Latin America; in Latin America, the Caribbean and Asia they form a large agricultural labour force. In sub-Saharan Africa, women's contribution to food production is as high as 73 per cent in some countries.[11] Despite their important role in ecological and agricultural rehabilitation and enduring food security, in many countries they do not have direct rights to land and their access to it is being curtailed by titles being provided to men. What little technology filters to peasants hardly reaches women; they form a tiny component of those peasants who receive training in modern methods; their traditional knowledge, especially regarding seed, is not sought nor built upon. They are not consulted regarding community forestry.

Labour Constraints: one of the problems facing resource-poor primary producers in Africa is the shortage of labour. Despite increasing populations, many rural households suffer from inadequate labour supplies as lack of rural development forces many young people to flock to urban areas. Yet labour is critical to food security. Historically, we know that apart from Japan, most industrialized countries raised labour productivity through technology. For many African countries, increased food production cannot be achieved in this way. Their economies simply cannot allow it. There are signs that instead of getting better, the economic situation in many countries will actually worsen over the next few decades. Therefore, labour must be retained in rural areas if agricultural productivity is to increase. Because of labour shortage, many rural old people, particularly women, have no option but to overcrop. Labour availability would help curtail overcropping and consequent degradation of soils. This means, then, that agricultural development generally and food security in particular are intimately linked to the question of rural development. With the possibility of securing a livelihood in rural areas, labour would remain there and augment the very low technology that many households apply.

Returns to labour: three distinct approaches to this can be seen in the three regions of the Developing World. In Africa, the stagnation of food production can be closely related to the stagnation of the smallholder sector. Smallholder production dominated by low returns from food crops in the shape of low product prices and lack of physical infrastructures, have contributed to marginalization and thus threaten food security. In Latin America and many Caribbean countries the inability of minifundia to support families has resulted in seasonal or permanent migration, while many landless people in Asia are absorbed into the agricultural labour force. In both cases, the returns are not sufficient to provide the purchasing power with which to meet food requirements.

Governments in developing countries will have to act quickly in developing curricula that will reflect local situations and productive sectors, particularly agriculture. All levels of education from primary to university, should have such curricula. At the same time, the value of outside education needs to be re-addressed. Countries must develop ways of retaining local and attracting non-local scientists, especially from other developing countries. By the same token, scientists must themselves be made aware of their country's or region's needs. Training and all the means to enhance the productivity of land should be specifically aimed at primary producers, especially peasants, and women among them, and as much as possible training should be carried out in situ with the producers themselves.

Land reforms should recognize women's crucial role in food production. Women should be given direct rights in land, especially where they are heads of households. They should be given as many educational opportunities as men. There should be more female extension workers to ensure that female farmers will have access to extension work; and women should participate in field visits. Women should have access to credit in their own right and there should be non-discriminatory access to inputs. Women's organizations should be promoted in decision-making regarding agricultural, including forestry, programmes.

Energy

Energy is an important input into agriculture, both directly as mechanical energy to pump water and move machines and vehicles, and indirectly in the form of fertilizers. At the same time, agriculture is an important means of producing energy through using biomass, in the form of fuelwood, agricultural and animal wastes, or feedstocks for more advanced conversion systems that produce ethanol, gas, electricity, etc. The agricultural system, therefore, has to be looked at as a user and a producer of energy, both of which are extremely important for development. A balance between the two is important, especially in countries where land is limited.

Agriculture is usually the least energy-intensive sector in national economies and the one with the highest economic and social returns for each extra unit of energy input. Regarding developing countries with low levels of modern energy-intensive inputs, it is hard to find examples where adding energy to the farming system is not profitable *in terms of extra yield and income.* By increasing yields or intensifying and extending the use of farmland, energy inputs also greatly increase employment, especially for the landless and other segments of rural populations who need work and frequently migrate to the cities to find it.

Globally, agriculture is a modest energy consumer, accounting for about 3.5 per cent of commercial energy use in industrial countries and 4.5 per cent in developing countries as a whole. A strategy to double food production in the developing countries through massive increases in fertilizers, irrigation and mechanization would add only 140 million tons of oil equivalent to their agricultural energy use. This is only some 5 per cent of present world energy consumption and almost certainly a small fraction of the energy that could be saved in other economic sectors. There is no global energy constraint on such an increase in energy consumption in developing countries' agriculture. But the difficulty for a particular energy-importing developing country to reallocate commercial energy (mainly oil) from other sectors to agriculture or to increase imports should not be underestimated. Even so, there is great scope for conservation and for improvements in efficiency in other sectors that could make additional energy sources available for agricultural purposes. In many cases now, the majority of the poor farmers will probably not have access to either the additional commercial energy supplies or the machines that would use these fuels.

There is, therefore, an urgent need for countries to explore different and more imaginative ways of producing sufficient energy locally, for use in agriculture, while at the same time not reducing levels of food production. There are vast possibilities both for large- and small-scale uses and individual countries and regions will have to work out what is most appropriate for them.

One of the most important energy-related needs is mechanical power for irrigation pumping. Many possibilities have been proved: windmills, conventional internal combustion engines running on biogas produced from local biomass wastes or on producer gas from the gasification of wood or charcoal. A number of developing countries command a substantial hydro-electricity potential. Where this has been developed, electric pumping provides advantageous options.

Post-harvest operations such as processing, storing and transporting also require energy. These are often neglected despite the fact that a substantial proportion of agricultural produce in developing countries becomes spoilt and deteriorates because of insufficient processing and storing equipment. In particular, solar dryers and solar coolers and refrigerators are very important and have been used extensively in some countries. Regarding transport, a great deal can be done with traditional animal-drawn carts for covering short distances. For longer distances, vehicles based on the well-proven internal combustion engine are the most efficient. In many places, it is possible to produce biofuels to run these engines. These would be based on locally available biomass sources, such as producer gas or alcohols. For stationary appliances (pumps or mills) it

35

is possible to use biogas to drive conventional diesel engines or electric generators.

In addition to providing energy for productive purposes, most of the above-mentioned technologies lend themselves to local design, development and production, even in countries with relatively low technological capabilities.

The use of renewable energy in agriculture is not, however, without problems. Distinction needs to be made between direct and indirect application of solar energy. The use of direct sunlight for crop drying and for evaporative "passive" cooling is more convincingly arguable than such indirect processes as photovoltaic cell convectors. The latter are still expensive and not very reliable in dusty climates. Experience with windmills is highly variable, as is biogas generation. Unfortunately, developing-country scientists and donors seem more intrigued by exotic forms of energy generation than by energy conservation. A heavy tax on gasoline for private vehicles in São Paulo, for example, would probably reduce significantly the need to use agricultural land for carbohydrates to be converted to ethanol.

Production of biomass-based fuels could lead to competition between food and energy production. This can take place even in areas where land is available. If the price is high enough, farmers will abandon food growing in favour of energy crops, as has happened in Brazil and in Gujarat, India. On the other hand, energy crops can be pursued if the returns are high enough to ensure economic access to food. Unless returns can ensure this, such changes will result in lowered access to food by the poor. Consequently, through appropriate pricing structures, as well as other actions, a careful balance can and must be kept between food and energy production.

The role of agroforestry systems must be emphasised here because they are so well suited for the production of food and fuel by small-scale and resource-poor farmers. In these systems, one or more tree crops are combined with one or more food crops or animal farming on the same plot of land in spatial or temporal combinations. If the different crops are well chosen, they reinforce each other and the total food and fuel production is greater than in separate food and fuel growing systems. Especially good results can be achieved by the use of multi-purpose trees in such agroforestry systems. Some tree species, such as acacia-albida can fix nitrogen and, consequently, fertilize the soil; some fruits are edible, while others are used as medicine; some leaves are used as animal fodder; and branches can be chopped off to provide firewood or to be used in basket making, etc.

Although the name is quite recent, agroforestry has been practised by traditional farmers everywhere. The challenge today is to revive the old methods and adapt them to the new conditions, in addition to developing new methods. Agroforestry practices can significantly reduce deforestation: they reduce the need to convert forest land into agricultural land and pastures and provide farmers with the means of producing their own firewood, timber, fertilizer, fodder, building poles and other forest products.

Fertilizers, Pesticides, Integrated Pest Management

Energy used in agriculture will increasingly be in the form of chemical control agents and fertilizers. In the short term, food production increases of 3 to 4 per cent a year cannot be achieved without an enormous increase in both. In the medium-term, these increases can be sustained only if they are managed so as to steadily reduce avoidable damage to soil, water, plants, animals and human health. Over-use and abuse of agro-chemicals impose heavy costs on a nation's economy and can quickly erode the ecological foundations of a thriving agro-ecosystem.

To date, this has represented more of a danger in developed than in developing countries, or so it has been assumed. Judging solely from past volumes of use, this seems a fair assumption. In 1978/79, developed countries used about three-quarters of world consumption of fertilizers and the US alone consumed over one-third of all pesticides used.

The balance is shifting rapidly, however, as it must in the interest of global food security. The use of fertilizers has been growing more than twice as fast in developing as in developed countries (averaging 10 per cent a year between 1969/70 and 1978/79) and the FAO projects future growth to the year 2000 at between 7.5 and 8 per cent per year,[12] twice the projected

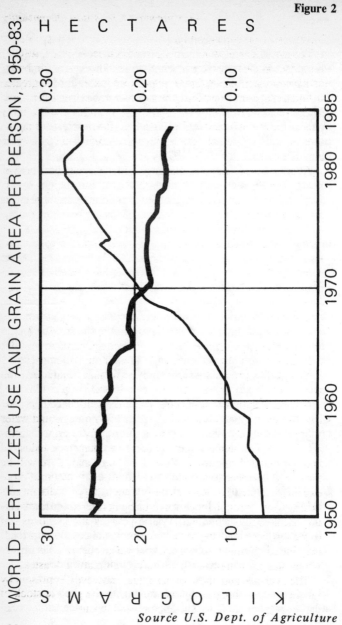

Figure 2

WORLD FERTILIZER USE AND GRAIN AREA PER PERSON, 1950-83.

HECTARES

KILOGRAMS

Source U.S. Dept. of Agriculture

increases in crop production.

The use of chemical control agents for insects, pests, weeds, fungi etc. is also growing at a rapid rate. If one superimposes on these projections the larger populations exposed, the greater institutional and educational barriers to safe use and the higher rates of inter-farm spill-overs stemming from the smaller farm pattern prevalent in developing countries, the problems of pollution and contamination could reach or exceed those of developed countries.

These problems manifest themselves in damage to both human health and the agricultural resource base. But they can also impact heavily on a nation's public expenditure, trade balance and debt burden.

Water resources are particularly sensitive to the run-off of nitrogen and phosphates from excess use of fertilizers. The process of eutrophication increases the burden on the water's limited supply of dissolved oxygen by stimulating the growth of aquatic plants. Eutrophication of large and small lakes, irrigation reservoirs, canals, and other water bodies has become a problem on a world-scale as it destroys fisheries and ruins major sources of water for drinking, recreation and other purposes. The feared death of the great lakes of North America and Europe brought the question to the international agenda in the mid-1960s. Although the process has been reversed in a few areas, the phenomenon has spread steadily ever since.

Nitrate pollution of water is a health hazard, particularly for infants, and the percolation of nitrogen into underground water sources can impose heavy costs on a community or region. Communities everywhere tap major aquifers for municipal, industrial and agricultural purposes. Many have been and more will be faced with the need to abandon these aquifers in favour of more expensive alternatives such as deeper wells, tapping distant surface supplies through pipelines or using bottled water for drinking. Ecologically blind agricultural policies and practices add to the fertilizer load and to the environmental costs of that load: they induce farmers to over-use and waste chemical fertilizers while making it more difficult to recycle natural wastes.

The over-use and abuse of pesticides, however, represent by far the greater threat to human health, to the genetic stock of the population and to sustainable and economically viable agriculture. Data are notoriously unreliable, but it is estimated that approximately 10,000 people die each year in developing countries and about 400,000 suffer acutely from pesticide poisoning. Most victims are farm workers, but accidental poisoning from food contamination is common.

A characteristic of many pesticides is that they become concentrated and magnified as they move up the food chain. The effects of chronic exposure to pesticide residues in food, water—even in the air—are global. The evidence is manifest in analyses of human tissue and mothers' milk. PCBs have been found in an impressive number of people in North America and Western Europe, while many lives are threatened in Eastern Europe and the USSR. In countries such as China and India where persistent organo-chlorine compounds are in use, medium concentrations in the fat of mothers' milk indicate that the milk consumed by breast-fed infants exceeds the danger limits established by WHO.

Unfortunately, little is known about the health effects of long-term exposure in populations, but the impact on some other species has been dramatic. Commercial fisheries have been destroyed, bird species endangered and predatory insects wiped out. Disrupting nature's ingenious balancing act by indiscriminate pesticide use has often served to increase the resistance of the target pests, while at the same time destroying natural predators. The number of pesticide resistant species worldwide jumped from 25 in 1974 to 432 in 1980.[13] Many resist even the newest chemicals. The variety and severity of pest infestations multiplies, threatening the very survival of agriculture in the areas concerned.

Making decisions about pesticide use is akin to dodging a boomerang. The risk of expensive crop losses increases the pressure to apply chemical control agents. Heavier applications accelerate the evolution of genetic resistance and create new pest problems as natural enemies are destroyed. The boomerang strikes when next year the risk of crop losses from new and tougher pests is balanced against the higher costs of increased applications of chemical control agents.

Ironically, in many countries, the difficult short-term risk-benefit balancing act is distorted by public subsidies, at great cost. After all, it is argued, pests must be controlled, on the farm and in storage; fertilizers must be applied in increasing volumes.

Are there no counter strategies? Or must society simply adapt to fisheries reduced by eutrophication, to underground aquifers sterilized by nitrate pollution, to ever higher deaths and injuries in developing countries from abuse of pesticides, to a losing battle against pests which themselves adapt faster than new chemicals can be invented, and eventually to lower yields, higher costs and reduced food security?

Adaptive strategies have their limits, but there is so much momentum in the present systems that they will doubtless prevail for some time. Alternative strategies are available that would gradually shift agriculture from almost exclusive dependence on persistent chemicals to *natural systems* of nutrient supply and pest control. They require a higher priority, however, and most of all, a change of public policies that now encourage the spread of chemical agriculture.

Means to control non-point sources of agricultural pollution are a case in point, especially the seepage of excess nutrients from fertilizers into water bodies. Solutions have so far escaped the ingenuity of policy planners, but then, the problems have not received much attention. Nitrate pollution of ground-water is another matter. Recharge areas for major aquifers can be identified. Moreover, while it may be difficult to deny farmers the right to apply fertilizers on such lands, the practice does not have to be subsidized from tax revenue, as it is in almost all developed and many developing countries. Indeed, perhaps farmers should be subject to a special tax to fund the increased water costs they will eventually impose on the community. Similarly, feed lots, a growing source of damage to surface waters, should be required to cover the costs of such damage. In this way, a value would be placed on animal wastes and their use as organic fertilizer would be encouraged.

The future is likely to see organic and inorganic sources of plant nutrients used increasingly to complement one another, with gradual and greater shifts to the former. Organic wastes such as crop residues are now commonly burnt in the fields and, as just noted, industrial feed lots have transformed farmyard manure from a solution into a problem. Such wastes are potentially significant sources of soil nutrients. Organic wastes are

41

also important low-cost soil conditioners. They reduce run-off, increase the take up of other nutrients and increase the water-holding and erosion-resistant capacity of the soil, qualities especially needed in the tropics. (Application of only two tons per hectare of organic mulch, for example, can reduce run-off by 80 per cent or more and reduce erosion by up to 95 per cent).

For many developing countries, organic fertilizers such as cattle or pig or chicken manure offer obtainable options because of their lower costs, especially when used alongside more resource-efficient cropping systems such as inter-cropping and rotation. Moreover, they are free from possible chemical contamination. More of this source of fertilizer could be developed communally or co-operatively. The overall systems-efficiency is particularly enhanced if the biomass feedstock (animal manure and/or other wet vegetable biomass) is anaerobically digested in biogas plants. In this process the potential health hazard of the original manure is destroyed. The slurry produced is an excellent fertilizer/soil conditioner. Moreover, in the process, biogas is formed, which can be used to run internal combustion engines in pumps, motors or electric generators. The process has potentials particularly in medium- to large-scale farm and agro-industrial units, where a sufficient number of animals is available for efficient operations. But it can also be well applied in small undertakings, for example in urban plots and kitchen gardens. The Maya farms in the Philippines is a good example of how a large agro-industrial complex is able to produce all its energy requirements and a great deal of its fertilizer requirements from animal manure through biogas plants.

Many more locally available sources of organic fertilizer can be more fully exploited. An additional 10 to 15 million tons of nitrogen and 5 million tons each of potassium and potash could be obtained in the developing countries if only half the available human and animal manure were used. In addition, a comprehensive composting or biogas programme throughout the developing countries could provide an estimated 50 to 100 million new jobs and provide more means for livelihood security.

In industrialized countries high energy prices could increase the attractiveness of organic farming, the technologies for which are becoming increasingly sophisticated and competitive. Studies in the UK, the US and the Netherlands have shown that organic food production can, when properly managed, produce up to 90 per cent of the yield per acre of conventional chemical agriculture at 66 per cent of the energy cost.[14] Anticipatory policies might be designed to support and even induce such a response.

Integrated pest management (IPM), initially employing an optimal combination of biological and chemical control technologies with gradual phasing out of the latter to rely on natural controls, is the most promising of the sustainable strategies for pest control. Because of the role of natural controls, IPM requires a decentralized ecosystem approach, however, with detailed information about individual pests, their environment, life cycles and natural enemies. Advances in genetic engineering offer great hope for IPM schemes, but their future depends more on institutional change than on technology. They require the awareness and full support of the farmers sharing an agro-ecosystem and the ability to modify farm practices to interrupt the life cycle of pests and aid their natural enemies. They require the development of seed varieties tailored to resist pests prevalent in different areas and integrated cropping patterns to reinforce this resistance. The implications of this for decentralized research linked to expanded locally generated extension services and supported strongly by national policy and international co-operation are evident.

Both organic recycling and IPM are labour intensive, a further attraction in developing countries needing to generate hundreds of millions of livelihoods in rural areas. They would reduce the need for inorganic fertilizers and pesticides, improve the balance of payments problem and release precious foreign exchange for other purposes. (Although developing countries as a group produced two-thirds of their fertilizer requirements in 1978-79—17.5 per cent of world output—this was concentrated in the oil exporting countries. This will remain true even if, as a group, they reach self-sufficiency by the turn of the century). Most developing countries must produce crops for export in order to pay for chemical fertilizers and pesticides. A study carried out in 1983 found that only 15 per cent of the money realized from developing countries' food exports reached the producing country. Commodity prices continue to fall—another

43

boomerang. Ten years ago, 10 tons of tea bought 17 tons of fertilizer; eight years later it bought 8 tons.[15]

While a greater reliance on non-chemical strategies is essential to the future of agriculture and development, a transition from existing strategies is not pre-ordained. Decision systems in agricultural as in other sectors, public and private, are structured to secure short-term gains at the expense of medium and long-term consequences. This process is reinforced by the fact that farmers seldom pay the full price for chemicals and fertilizers, and almost never pay the damage costs to human health and the environment. These are passed on to others, downstream or downwind, or to the taxpayer.

The transition will take place only if certain key distortions in the decision systems are reversed. Several pre-conditions must be met. In the first place, the legislative and institutional framework for controlling and regulating agro-chemicals must be greatly strengthened. In developed countries, where such systems are already in place, this means ensuring that the legal institutions are not subordinate to ministers and senior officials whose overriding aim is to increase next year's yield. In developing countries, it means much more. Although perhaps half of the developing countries have some basic legislation, in most of them the importation, production, transport, use and disposal of pesticides are virtually not controlled. All developing countries must possess the basic legislative and institutional instruments to manage the agro-chemical age within their countries. However, new forms of international support are also necessary. This is the case because of the international nature of the agro-chemical industry, the fact that most developing countries are almost totally dependent on imports and because of the inherent weakness of their institutions.

The second pre-condition is that the legislative, policy and research capacity for advancing non-chemical strategies must be established and sustained. The most important single step should be to redesign the subsidy systems that now induce farmers to over-use and abuse chemical fertilizers and pesticides, as discussed above. These are most elaborate in developed countries, but are also found in some developing countries. In a study undertaken for the Commission in eight developing countries, pesticide subsidies were found to be widespread and substantial, significantly affecting farmers' decisions concerning their use. They also represent a heavy drain on the treasury, in some cases exceeding expenditures on health, housing and water supply. The impact on the balance of payments and the drain on foreign currency is also substantial. No similar programmes seem to exist to encourage non-chemical strategies.

Urban Agriculture

Historically, urban dwellers in industrialized countries faced severe food insecurity during periods of crisis such as war. The activity of growing food in pots, on windowsills, balconies and in small backyard plots was seen as an important source of food and took on a new dimension. In the US during World War II, for example, "victory gardens" provided 40 per cent of the fresh vegetables. At present, some families in Western cities have garden allotments, mainly vegetables but also for poultry and small ruminants such as rabbits and guinea pigs. This supplements the food budgets for some of the needy. In the majority of cases the loss of this resource would make little difference to financial security. To these people a driving force for kitchen gardening is a "green thumb" or the desire to be free of food contamination through chemicals.

In many developing countries, however, so far as many of the urban poor are concerned, their sources of livelihood, including the ability to command food, are steadily being eroded. Acknowledging this, some local authorities have been encouraging urban agriculture.

The major constraint has been the availability of land; some governments have been attempting to reclaim unoccupied land for this purpose. Others have been urging a new approach to urban expansion by setting aside some land specifically for urban agriculture or allotting bigger plots to meet housing and gardening requirements. Future urban development should take this source of food security into account by providing adequate access to land, clean water and other inputs.

As Dana Silk puts it in "Urban Agriculture" (1985):[16] "At least 85 per cent of the vegetables consumed by urban residents in China are produced within the urban municipalities. The

45

megalopolises of Shanghai (population 11 million) and Peking (population 8 million) are 100 per cent self-sufficient in vegetable production using nationally established production goals. Fish, small animal and tree-crop production are also intensive activities in Chinese cities and important sources of protein for urban residents.

"Both Hong Kong and Singapore have significant urban agriculture programmes. Hong Kong produces almost half of its fresh vegetable consumption and almost three-quarters of its poultry consumption, while Singapore produces 100 per cent of its pork consumption, 80 per cent of its chickens, 30 per cent of its fish and 27 per cent of its fresh vegetables.

"In the Papua New Guinea city of Lae, the municipally sponsored garden allotments have been so successful that surplus produce is bought by the City to provide subsidized "nutri-pies" for school children.

"The African city of Lusaka, Zambia, has been the subject of considerable effort in this regard, where a national Urban Agriculture and Nutrition Service has been established to facilitate the formation of community co-operatives for the purchase of seeds, fertilizers and tools to complement the provision of land.

"In Addis Ababa, municipal land has also been provided to the poor for gardening purposes. In Cairo, one of the most densely populated cities in the world, it is estimated that 5 per cent of the women raise small livestock and thus provide their families with valuable protein source."

Overall, in developing countries urban agriculture helps cities recycle organic waste, as in Lae, by actually reducing solid waste disposal needs by 10 per cent; reduces energy cost incurred through processing and transportation; and meets poor people's nutritional needs. In many poor families where food accounts for 50 to 70 per cent of the total monthly family income, kitchen gardening saves 10 to 20 per cent of the total food budget.

Preserving and Enhancing the Quality of the Existing Resource Base

Enduring food security will depend on a sustainable and productive resource base. The challenge facing governments and producers is to increase agricultural productivity and thus ensure food security, while enhancing the productive capacity of this natural resource base in a sustainable manner. Land and water degradation pose the most formidable threats to the resource base. The degradation results from non-sustainable land use and poor irrigation. It is imperative to develop land and water management systems which will reverse the current pressures on the environment and the consequent degradation of the soils; at the same time, these should ensure that there are no further degradation-related pressures.

Deforestation

Forests and their ecosystems constitute a fundamental factor of stability. Their destruction or conversion can exert serious long-term effects on the biosphere, particularly on the ecology, hydrometeorology, hydrology and on the human, animal and plant life they support. Indeed, the widespread droughts that have so tragically affected Africa over the past two decades can be directly attributed to the indiscriminate removal of the protecting and nurturing forest vegetation in many parts of that continent. Although this destruction or conversion has been taking place in an unprecedented manner throughout the world, today the greatest challenge to forests and woodlands is to be found in developing countries, particularly in their rain forests. This century has seen a reduction of forests by almost a half; every year 11.3 million ha. are destroyed.

Some Causes Of Deforestation

The causes of deforestation in developing countries are complex and deeply rooted in the patterns of their developmental evolution. The inequitable distribution of land, the marginalization of the majority of the poor, rapid population growth, unregulated timber exploitation, agricultural and ranching expansion, the demands for fuelwood, non-existent or inadequate forest

47

policies, unscientific forest management and the absence of overall land-use plans have all contributed to the diminution of the forest estate in the developing world and to the tragedies that have, in consequence, occurred.

Timber Exploitation: many countries endowed with large forest resources have come to regard their forests as sources of foreign exchange. There is, of course, nothing intrinsically wrong with a policy that seeks to utilize a resource so that it contributes to general development. In practice, however, although in some countries small numbers of local industries have been established, more often than not the wood is exported in its unprocessed form and the value added through its subsequent industrial conversion accrues in the developed countries. In addition, the revenues that are paid to the governments of the developing countries for the right to exploit their forests are often derisory. Not only are they low when compared to those paid in the developed world, but when account is taken of the damage caused to the general forests through the selective logging of mixed tropical hardwoods, the returns to developing countries are, in most cases, negative. In other words, in purely economic terms, governments are subsidizing the timber companies.

Perhaps more important than these immediately apparent economic losses is the degradation that often occurs in fragile forest ecosystems. Forests are cleared from steep hills, in areas of high rainfall intensities,and from soils that are extremely erodible. The inevitable result is the erosion of the topsoil, the reduction of the capacity of the soil to retain water, increased water run-off, a greater liability to floods in the rainy seasons and an enhanced propensity to drought in the dry seasons. Rivers and costly irrigation schemes are subject to siltation; downstream agriculture is adversely affected, and there is famine.

Agricultural and Ranching Expansion: another cause of forest depletion in developing countries has been the opening up of forests for agricultural production and for ranching. This is especially important in Latin America (although it occurs elsewhere also) where big landowners lock up vast areas of forest. In addition, because of increasing populations and the growing unavailability of arable land capable of sustaining agricultural production without additional inputs, many poor farmers seek new lands in the forests to grow more food. They have done this for many millennia with little or no permanent deterioration of the ecosystems. However, as populations grow more rapidly and as the areas of forests dwindle, they are now forced to return to the same areas of land much more quickly than they did in the past. The result is not only that the abandoned land is not given adequate time to recover before being subjected to another round of farming, but the rate of soil depletion increases exponentially. Indeed, in some parts of Africa deforestation caused by shifting cultivation is 40 times higher than that caused by forest exploitation for fuelwood. And in Latin America, shifting cultivation accounts for 33 per cent of annual deforestation. Other small local farmers and landless squatters add to forest denudation.

Government policies encourage these developments, indirectly through marginalization and directly through settlement programmes. The Government of Indonesia, for example, is implementing a programme to settle people from over-populated Java in the outer islands. If the programme is efficiently carried out, 3 million ha. representing 5 per cent of the productive forests will have been converted to agriculture by 1988.[17] By the year 2000, a great extent of forest area will be highly threatened if projected rates are successfully completed. In Brazil huge areas have been converted for use by small-scale farmers and big owners. There is nothing inherently wrong with extending agriculture in this way. In point of fact, future food security in developing countries will depend to a large extent on bringing additional arable land under cultivation. But are these the best lands? Has the capacity of the forest soils to sustain agricultural production been assessed? In some cases the soils of converted lands are poor in nutrients, most of which are held in the biomass or the top inch or two of the soil. Moreover, unless these settlement exercises are linked and integrated with the management of the forests, it is possible that they will result in more long-term harm than good.

Ranching is another activity that has contributed significantly to deforestation. Indeed, in Central America it has been the major cause of forest depletion. There, man-made pasturelands have increased by two-thirds since 1960 while forests declined by 40 per cent between 1961-78. National governments, anxious to find ways of earning foreign exchange, have accordingly encouraged and supported ranching. The conversion from forest to pasture was stimulated by the need for cheaper sources of beef to meet the demand for fast foods in the US—hamburgers in this case. Brazil is another example of government-supported ranching encroachment into forestland. In 1980, government-subsidized ranches contributed four times as much to deforestation as did non-subsidized projects. And the latter are quite impressive. Worldwide, ranching is estimated to deforest about 20,000 km^2 every year, Latin America being responsible for the largest portion.

Fuelwood: wood comprises the major source of energy in developing countries, where in many cases, it accounts for 50 per cent or more of total national energy use. Persisting high fossil-energy prices and deteriorating economic performance have forestalled any attempts to introduce or substitute commercial energy; in fact they have accelerated dependence on fuelwood. To develop action-oriented, target-specific and appropriate strategies and policies, it is essential to get a clearer picture of the demand, supply and end-users. There are two main use sectors: rural and urban domestic use; rural and urban processing and small-scale industries. Households are the largest consumers, accounting for over 80 per cent in the majority of countries.

For Rural Domestic Use: the per person firewood consumption varies within and between countries, although comprehensive documentation of this is inadequate. Scanty data for Africa and Asia demonstrate that the mean firewood use of 1.42 m^3/capita/annum in rural Africa is higher than that of rural Asia where it is 0.83 m^3. Most African countries with extensive semi-arid zones (for example, the Sudan, Mali, Niger, Tunisia, Lesotho and Botswana) have lower rural per capita firewood consumption than the mean of 1.42 m^3 for Africa. This indicates the severity of the rural firewood scarcity in Asia and the semi-arid countries of Africa. Charcoal is rarely used in rural areas, although in rural Africa this accounts for about 34 per cent of total fuelwood consumption. As a higher proportion of rural fuelwood requirements is supplied by collecting dead wood in natural forests or by wood cut during cropland clearing, the contribution of rural domestic requirements to deforestation is relatively insignificant.

In spite of the massive investments in urban electrification, the majority of urban households in developing countries depend on fuelwood for cooking and heating. In some countries, for example Mozambique, Somalia, Tanzania, The Gambia and Mali, 65 to 100 per cent of urban household fuelwood use is in the form of firewood; in others, such as Kenya, Thailand and Zambia, charcoal accounts for 60 to 80 per cent of total urban household energy. In Africa the mean total fuelwood consumption of 3.09 m^3/person/annum in urban areas is higher than that of 1.42 m^3/person/annum in rural areas. In the past, when forests were available in the vicinity of cities, households collected their own fuelwood supplies. But the high urban population growth rate, which is 2 to 3 times that of rural populations and the consequent spatial expansion of cities has led to the denudation of natural forests around urban areas. Now, the bulk of fuelwood is obtained through commercial channels. Throughout the developing world, there are thousands of woodcutters in the countryside who clear-cut live trees to produce fuelwood for sale in urban areas. The supply of urban fuelwood is a major cause of deforestation for two main reasons: wood for sale and for making charcoal involves clear-cutting of live trees; and the traditional technology for converting wood to charcoal in earth kilns requires two to three times as much wood to deliver the same amount of useful energy as firewood.

Rural based and processing industries such as pottery and beer brewing use wood but they do not consume as much as those industries that process commercial crops (tobacco, tea or coffee). For example, tobacco drying in Tanzania has been responsible for the massive deforestation in the Tabora region. Nationally, tobacco produced on one hectare requires clear-cutting of a hectare of woodland. In Zambia, it requires 37 tons of dry wood to produce one ton of flue-cured tobacco. Tobacco curing and rubber preparation consumed 300,000 m^3 of fuelwood in Thailand in 1970. Fish processing has also contributed significantly to indigenous deforestation. In the Sahel, the drying of a ton of fish requires 3.25 tons of wood, which may have to be transported from as far as 100 km away. Unlike the collection of household fuelwood, fuel energy for rural industries involves the cutting and often clear-cutting of live trees. Consequently, it is a significant cause of deforestation. Regarding wood as a free good, these industries rarely, if ever, pay for cutting live trees, hardly exercise any stewardship of the forest resources, and are, therefore, often wasteful of the resource.

Urban and industrial enterprises add considerably to the demands for urban fuelwood. In Kenya, industries and commercial enterprises account for as much as 23 per cent of the fuelwood demand. In Central America, they are estimated to account for 18 per cent of the total fuelwood demand. In Brazil, charcoal supplies 40 per cent of the energy needs of the steel industry. The copper industry in Zambia uses some 20,000 tons of charcoal annually as a reducing agent in its copper refineries. Most urban industries, like urban households, purchase their fuelwood from rural producers or urban fuelwood merchants and syndicates.

It is not surprising that many developing countries face energy crises. As forests recede, rural people, especially women, have to walk several kilometres a day in search of fuelwood. The burden this places on them dictates the number and quality of their meals and threatens nutritional security. When fuelwood is scarce they must turn to using other biomass, such as animal and agricultural wastes, thus depriving food production of these inputs. In 1980, the FAO estimated that 100 million people in developing countries were not able to satisfy their minimum fuelwood needs. At the same time the minimum energy needs of a further 1,050 million (mainly urban) were being met through overcutting the wood resources. A 1984 World Bank report on the Sahel has identified fuelwood needs as one area where the man/resource base ratio is beyond the carrying capacity.[18]

Greater and sustainable efforts are needed at the policy and action levels to reverse this phenomenon. To this end, social forestry programmes that are already under way but falling short of even the required minimum should be strengthened. They can, however, only be successfully implemented through the active participation of the local communities at all stages and levels. Decision-makers should, therefore, provide the frameworks that will enable grassroots people to identify the extent of their needs and discuss with them what is needed by way of land, seedlings and other inputs. To the rural people, forests are a source of many aspects of livelihood: soil fertility, fuelwood, medicines, food and shade, among others. As the more directly affected victims of deforestation, they also make better custodians, as the Chipko Movement in India has demonstrated. Some responsibility for managing the existing and degraded natural forests should, therefore, be devolved to them. Greater action is required by governments and the international community in the following five fields to augment previous efforts in fuelwood programmes:

1. training and research in social forestry, agro-forestry and the management of natural forests;
2. establishment of green belts to meet urban needs;
3. expansion or establishment of nurseries for seedling production, close enough to settlements to respond to demands and to ensure participation;
4. improvement of existing charcoal-conversion production techniques and introduction of others; and
5. promotion of fuel-efficient stoves, especially in urban areas.

In addition and where possible, users should be encouraged to adopt other renewable sources of energy.

We have concentrated on developing countries in our treatment of the destruction of forests primarily because, although the expansion of agriculture, urbanization and industrialization has in the past contributed to the removal and depletion of a proportion of the forests in the now industrialized countries, sound forest management evolved early enough to save a fair amount of their natural forests. Moreover, their financial and technological resources have enabled them to replace many of the forests that had been removed with more efficient plantations and to restore a significant proportion through natural regeneration processes. It is our opinion that although there may be a few industrialized countries in which there is still forest depletion, the areas involved are so small that they do not in themselves warrant international concern. In addition, when viewed from a global perspective, temperate forests do not possess a great diversity of genetic resources. At present, forests in some countries are threatened as a result of *inter alia* acid

53

rain, but developed countries possess the capacity and knowledge to control the incidence of this phenomenon if they wish collectively so to do.

The Effects Of Deforestation

The effects of deforestation can be far-reaching: indigenous forest dwellers and forest-based economies are sometimes displaced; a valuable development and renewable resource capable of assisting in the process of industrialization, in absorbing labour and in earning foreign exchange is destroyed; soils are degraded; water regimes which depend upon the existence of the forests are upset; and many wildlife species lose their habitats. Human suffering and loss of human productivity are also caused by the receding forests. For example, in certain rural areas great hardships have been placed on women who must now walk for long distances, often for 38 hours per week, to collect fuelwood and fodder. In urban areas, wood scarcity pushes up prices to levels which the main users, who are already impoverished, can hardly afford. In some parts of Haiti where a modicum of food is produced, people still go hungry because there is no fuel to cook it with. To these immediate results of deforestation are added the long term effects on food security, to which we now turn.

Genetic Resources: in recent years science has made strides which promise to extend man's ability to alter plants and animals to make them more useful to society. Indeed, the importance of genetic diversity has long been recognized in sustaining and improving agricultural productivity. Already genetic improvements have resulted in increased agricultural yields in the industrialized countries and Asia. It is this growing knowledge of the usefulness of genetic resources that creates concern for the wanton destruction of their habitats. Species diversity increases from the temperate to the tropical regions. Thus Jamaica, with an area only 4 per cent that of Britain has a flora that is one-and-a-half times greater in number of species; and Kenya has three times the number of breeding species of land birds that France and Switzerland possess together. Within the tropics, the moist forests have the highest number of both plant and animal species. While they cover only 7 per cent of the earth's land area, they harbour 40 to 50 per cent of all animal species and some 100,000 of those of the higher plants.

The magnitude of the threat to this resource is brought home by the rate of tropical deforestation. Unfortunately, we do not have reliable figures for the current extinction rates of invertebrates and plant species, but the extinction rate for flowering plants is known to be extremely high. Indeed, it has been stated that should the present rate of deforestation continue, more than 50 per cent of the higher plant species will be extinct by the year 2000. Moreover, most of the domesticated crop plants and animals originated in the so-called Vavilov centres of genetic diversity, located in developing countries. Today, they are distinguished by marked germ-plasm diversity of the cultivars. These are being lost under modern processes and habitat change. For example, African centres of domestication (Barbary, Sudan-Sahel, Ethiopia, East African highlands, West-Central forest belt) are all areas experiencing marked environmental stress and modification.

Clearly, campaigns now in progress to conserve the biota in situ are a matter of priority for national governments. In addition, efforts to preserve the biota as germ-plasm *ex situ* in banks must be increased as a matter of urgency for the future of sustainable agriculture. Seed collection being urged by organizations such as the International Board of Plant Genetic Resources should receive greater co-operation through the establishment of national and regional laboratories to preserve all local genetic material. Governments should themselves encourage plant breeders to step up their collections of adaptive genes of major crops for local use.

Soil Degradation: forests physically protect the soil and maintain its nutrient status at one and the same time. Physical protection is attained through the stratified physiognomy of forests, which reduces the impact of falling rain upon the soil beneath and thus minimizes erosion and soil loss. This "above ground effect" is further supported by the cushions of litter and humus that are found on the floor of natural and well-managed forests. Forest soil fertility is maintained because forests return most of the nutrients they take out of the soil through a cyclical process of nutrient uptake and deposition. The forests are therefore a self-perpetuating nutrient factory. With their removal, this self-sustaining process is broken. It is therefore not surprising that in many parts of the world where forests have been removed, soil degradation and lower productivity have been recorded as, for example, in Mexico, Colombia, Peru and Ecuador and in whole regions of Africa.

Fortunately, in many cases, the position can be reversed through reforestation and controlled through the curtailment of further deforestation. Unfortunately, the establishment of forest plantations is not only relatively costly, but the returns on the investment incurred in establishing them are somewhat delayed because of the long gestation periods of tree crops. In these circumstances, where there is population pressure on the land, agro-forestry systems should be practised. Where possible, multi-purpose leguminous species should be planted. These would not only enrich the soil but would provide a range of products that could be of use to the rural populations.

Climatic Change: forests influence local climates. For example, the forests that stretch from the humid region of West Africa to the Congo and follow the Atlantic coast of Africa from Liberia to the mouth of the Congo, form a humidity belt for the ocean monsoon as it moves towards Central Africa. The drylands of the Sahel get their humidity and their water, in the dry season, from the ocean and the thick coastal forests which extend the influence of the sea towards the centre of the continent. If these forests were removed, their regulating influence on rainfall might be affected. Whether tropical deforestation can effectively disrupt the stability of world climates remains controversial. There are strong indications, however, that when forests are removed, more solar heat is reflected back into space (the "albedo" effect). Many scientists believe that this can lead to changes in global patterns of air circulation, with a potential impact on agriculture.

Upland Watersheds: disruptions of the ecosystem are more acutely felt in upland watersheds. The uplands play a very important role in the hydrological cycle: they influence the precipitation of moisture in the form of snow or rain; at the global macroscale, the water-distribution system can be viewed as resulting from the interaction of dominating winds from evaporation centres in the ocean and the high mountain ranges that induce precipitation. Observations have shown that precipitation is much higher in the mountains than in the lowlands. As an example, the Himalayas cause rain in the hills and influence the rainfall in the plains. A numerical simulation model with and without the inclusion of mountain topography in South Asia has shown that in the absence of the Himalayas, the continental low pressure belt would shift to extreme North-East China and a desert-like climate would be created in South Asia as the result of dry continental air flowing from the northwest.

Uplands are also the source of all major river systems of the world and provide the potential energy for the maintenance of flow in streams and rivers in the plains. Since the stability of the water flow is largely a function of the state of the soil-vegetation system, the most stable upland watersheds are those where there has been the least human intervention and where the natural vegetation is adapted to local microclimatic variation and acts as an instrument in soil and water stabilization. On the other hand, destabilization changes the flow characteristics of the streams and rivers in terms of the distribution of the yield and seasonality.

Deforestation, especially of tropical forests, has had this destabilizing effect. Floods and droughts occurring everywhere are linked to the deforestation and consequent destabilization of upland watersheds. In the words of one peasant farmer in Zambia:

> These (charcoal traders) are the causes of our problems. They have denuded the whole area from village A to village B of vegetation cover. As a result we had more intense drought two years ago; last year the area was flooded. Producers could not produce and our children went hungry.[19]

and the Chipko Movement slogan:

> What do forests bear?
> Soil, water and pure air.[20]

Yet the local populations who make such wise utterances do not control their resources. In almost all cases these are controlled by governments which formulate policies and allow practices that undermine the forest resource base. For any forestry programme to be successful it must attempt to conserve the ecosystem while at the same time contributing to the developmental process. In other words, it must try to reconcile the apparently conflicting demands of the conservationist and the developer. It must also be more people oriented and consciously take into account the local grassroots people who are sometimes both the victims and agents of destruction. They should be the centre of the policies and management practices, which we adumbrate in the following section.

Forest Policy, Land Classification And Forest Management
It should be stated quite clearly that we do not consider all forests to be inviolable. Forests play important roles in soil protection, in maintaining soil fertility, in regulating water supplies, in influencing microclimates and in contributing to various aspects of development. The pursuit of these many faceted, and sometimes conflicting goals, should be based on scientific analyses. First, the inherent capacity of the land under forests to perform various functions should be ascertained: soil analyses should be conducted, topographic surveys made and detailed climatic studies undertaken in order to formulate a land capacity classification. This should provide the basis for future land utilization. Scientific land capacity classification would reveal which land would need to be under forest cover and which could be used for various other types of economic activity. Where there is population pressure and where all the land is inherently unsuitable for sustained agriculture, agro-forestry systems, which conserve the ecosystem and at the same time produce food, will have to be followed. Even when an area is suitable for forestry and forestry is being practised, the forests should be managed scientifically in such a way that their productivity is sustained. In addition, wherever possible, the forests should be managed in an integrated manner. The objectives of integrated management would be to maintain the ecosystem; to offer better socio-economic options that would lead to an adequate and acceptable quality of life for those who depend upon the ecosystems, and at the same time to maintain biological diversity.

On the basis of the land capability classification, the integrated management of forests might provide: a portion of land for annual crops under intensive cultivation, a portion for permanent crops, a portion for livestock, low-quality land for agro-forestry and, where necessary, areas devoted exclusively to the provision of such forest services as water regulation, etc. It must also be understood that many forests can be used to provide, at one and the same time, a multiplicity of both goods and services. Often there is no need to manage forests on a single-purpose basis. It cannot be too strongly emphasized that the degree of management integration and the number of uses to which a particular forest area will be subject will depend ultimately upon the results of the scientific analysis made of the forests, soils, topography and climate.

Such an approach would obviously entail changes in the way development priorities are set by the affected governments and greater devolution of responsibilities to local governments and communities. National governments will have to include environmental conservation in all development programmes; population policies will have to be readdressed as will rural development strategies; land ownership will have to be re-evaluated and reforms implemented and land be rendered more productive; reforestation of low-grade lands no longer suitable for agriculture or husbandry will have to be accelerated. Existing treaties will have to be re-negotiated to ensure sustainability of forest exploitation and overall environmental and ecosystem conservation. Prices for forest produce will have to reflect the actual and environmental value of the products.

All this will have to be underpinned by solid research. We strongly urge that international forestry research organizations be established as soon as possible, in various tropical countries in selected ecosystems, along the lines now followed by the Consultative Group for International Agricultural Research (CGIAR) and where they exist, e.g. the International Council for Research on Agro-Forestry (ICRAF), they should be strengthened and included in CGIAR networks. These research organizations should undertake work specifically in agro-forestry and should attempt to develop models that will foretell more precisely what will be the effect on water and soil loss, for example, of removing portions of forest cover in specific locations. The inter-relationships of forests and agriculture should also be examined in these organizations, and the role of forestry in increasing agricultural production should be given greater emphasis in research. We hold the view that forestry is the branch of agriculture with great potential for increasing productivity through improved regeneration practices, tissue culture, species composition, harvesting practices, utilization, etc. This potential will not be attained unless systematic research is undertaken through a network of well-staffed and adequately funded forest research centres.

Water And Food Security

The availability of good quality water in adequate quantities at the appropriate time determines the productivity and sustainability of agriculture, forestry and fishing and hence, has a profound significance on global food security. Six per cent of the earth's surface is classified as extreme desert and a further 29 per cent as subject to varying degrees of desertification hazards. Taking these facts into account and given the limitations of rainfed agriculture on account of unpredictable precipitation periods, we can say that any expansion in area and intensity in agricultural production will require intensified but sustainable management of the land-water-vegetation system. This in turn implies dramatic adjustments in current modes of withdrawal, delivery and management of water. It implies, too, action to reduce the stress factors (deforestation, desertification, soil erosion, population growth etc.). Globally, over 70 per cent of the fresh water withdrawal from the hydrological cycle for human use goes into irrigation.

Irrigation

It is generally estimated that around 13 to 14 per cent of the world's available lands are irrigated—about 223 million ha.— and need approximately 1,400 billion cubic metres of water. Half of the irrigated area came under irrigation during the last 20 to 30 years. The current growth rate for irrigated land is estimated at 2.9 per cent per year compared to 0.7 per cent per year for non-irrigated land. Whatever the statistical uncertainties, there is general agreement among agronomists that more land must be irrigated if food production is to increase. The International Food Policy Research Institute has estimated that three-fifths of the food increases, if projected for all developing countries over the next decade, will result from extending land under irrigation.

The critical role irrigation plays in food security has been demonstrated. To give a few examples: the dramatic rise in Indian grain production in the late 1960s was due as much to irrigation as to improved seeds, while China's production increases recorded over the last five years are due substantially to irrigation. In Mexico more than half of the total commercial farm output measured in monetary terms comes from land under irrigation, although only 30 per cent of the cropland is irrigated. In the irrigated Japanese rice culture, 0.045 ha. of land suffices to provide 2,500 ha., whereas in the US, twice as much land is needed for the same purpose. By contrast, rainfed agriculture dominates Africa with irrigated land amounting to only 3 per cent; thus only 15.7 per cent of its potential irrigation area is used. If this was exploited, yields would increase 24-fold.

While improvements in rainfed agriculture will result in limited increases, major emphasis will have to be on improving existing schemes, extending the area under irrigation and improving the management of irrigated water.

The Ill Effects of Irrigation: the role of irrigation in increasing yields is not in question. What is in question is its sustainability and socio-economic effects. Three main ill effects are discernible.

First, a number of irrigation systems did not take the human aspect into consideration. Two main adverse consequences may be noted in this connection: a) diseases arising from the prevalence of water-borne, water-based and water-related vectors; and b) socio-economic disruption. The increased disease, malnutrition and social unrest stemming from both are widely publicized. Farmers who lose all or part of their cropland, and in some cases livestock, rarely get fair compensation for their losses. Where they do, the amount of funding for recompense is negligible when compared to total project funding cost, yet it is so crucial since each farm family has few sources of non-farm income. Failure to recognize this factor makes planning deficient in this most basic and humanistic sense. In some cases, implementation of new irrigation systems causes changes in the socio-economic functions of the project area, especially if previous irrigation experience is lacking. Conversion from

61

rainfed agriculture to irrigation forces farmers to master quickly difficult new methods, which are often quite contrary to traditional practices. Moreover, change in water-use patterns and priorities can cause tensions and hostilities. The amount of energy required for irrigation is an important socio-economic concern. When energy was relatively inexpensive, equipment and pumps were often over-sized to provide a margin of safety. Now, with persistent high consumer energy costs, farmers must carry a much heavier burden for the wasted energy or make expensive conversions to more energy-efficient equipment.

Secondly, irrigation projects may have an impact on plants and animals well beyond the area circumscribed by project boundaries. Irrigation always removes some habitats of the native species but, in general, it tends to favour the most aggressive plant and animal species. Plants with numerous and highly mobile seeds are able to take advantage of the improved soil moisture and fertility of irrigated fields. Those with reproductive adaptations which depend on the peculiarities of arid or semi-arid climates for germination, will no longer flourish within the constantly moist fields.

Thirdly, the greatest threat to sustainable food security is salinization. Waterlogging, secondary salinization and alkalization result from ill-designed and poorly implemented irrigation systems. It appears that this is one of the areas where humankind has failed to draw lessons. Throughout history, salinity has been turning once-productive soils into non-productive or less-productive areas. FAO and UNESCO estimates show that as much as half of all existing irrigation schemes of the world are more or less under the influence of salinization, alkalization and waterlogging. These estimates translate to a global abandonment of some 10 million ha. irrigated land annually. At present, no continent using irrigation schemes in the conduct of its agriculture has been able to escape from the occurrence of salinization. In Argentina, nearly 50 per cent of the irrigated lands show signs of salinization. A survey carried out in Pakistan in 1965 showed that one-seventh of the irrigated land was salinized after a few years; in 1980, 40 per cent of the irrigated areas in Iraq and Iran were similarly affected. The Nile Delta is exhibiting degradation in this once very fertile area. The area is plagued with problems of salinity, and alkalinity (in addition to a rising water table, and industrial and chemical pollution caused by fertilizers and pesticides). In Australia salinization and alkalization are taking place in the Valley of the River Murray; in Northern Victoria about 80,000 ha. have already been affected. Alberta, Canada and the northern states of the US are experiencing similar stresses.[21]

More of the above effects can be avoided if substantial research is carried out in the planning and execution stages of the scheme. The aims of the research would be:

1. to measure the amount of the soil at the beginning and at the end of the project;
2. to measure the rate of leaking; and
3. to measure the rate of accumulation in the soil.

Integrated Water Management

The social and economic implications of the above adverse effects of irrigation call for the most effective land-water management systems. Integrated water-land management, taking into account the ecological, biological, social and economic factors, should be a priority concern. In designing irrigation projects, the role of watersheds, potential for aquaculture, provision of drinking water, navigation and transport possibilities should also be integrated, while emphasizing the primary objective of water for crop irrigation.

An earlier section demonstrated how integrated forest management can contribute to integrated water management. Special care must be exercised not to disrupt watersheds and generally to desist from wanton destruction of forests. More could be gained by the design and execution of irrigation systems themselves. It is accepted by most experts in industrialized countries (Canada, US) and in some developing countries such as Mexico that big dams are no longer possible. Whatever the reasons for this realization, it is moving irrigation in the right direction. In developing countries it may well be economically and socially desirable to convert large systems to cater for the needs of small farmers. Conversion has an added advantage of causing less disruption to the local populations and economies. Where irrigation systems have not been developed, as in much of Africa, there must be a shift in emphasis away from major reservoir-based irrigation toward small-tank/reservoir mine irrigation. This has the added advantage of involving the local people in planning, designing, construction and direction. Chances of diseases are also minimized. The socio-economic interests of people, the supposed beneficiaries, would be assured on a more sustainable basis. In addition, the climatic, ecological, economic, social and political factors have to be thoroughly examined and established for irrigation schemes to be of long-term advantage.

Fisheries: aquaculture

Proper and integrated water management provides options for sustainable development of fisheries and aquaculture generally. This development is critical to livelihood security because fisheries, especially inland fisheries and aquaculture, are a source of both protein and employment, particularly during the off-season for rural farmers. On the average, over 6 per cent of the total protein content of the human diet comes from fish and other aquatic products and accounts for nearly 17 per cent of the total animal protein intake. However, these averages conceal substantial differences between and within countries. Thirty-two, mainly poor, countries get 34 per cent or more of their animal protein from seafood, while another 11 countries consume double the world average. In some West and East African countries, fish provides 50 per cent or more of the animal protein. Of the total food projections by the turn of the century, 10 to 15 per cent is expected to come from marine and inland fisheries. In addition to this important nutritional intervention, exports of fishery products (fish meal, tinned fish, etc.) generate valuable foreign exchange, which in turn some countries use to import more food. Moreover, the small-scale fisheries can and do provide wage employment. Fisheries are also ecologically benign and, in fact, can help restore the soils. In efforts to rehabilitate the ecology, therefore, fisheries can contribute to land reclamation.

Inland fisheries could also be efficient in making use of less productive soils. In some countries, for example Sierra Leone, where mineral prospectors have left many holes in the ground, these could be turned into ponds and thus bring what would otherwise be wastelands into production.

Fresh water and marine fisheries have the economic advantage of yielding the highest return per hectare and there are indications that this will improve or at least be retained over the next decades. In 1982, fresh water fisheries landed around 8 million tons: catches in Asia accounted for 70 per cent of this total with 14 per cent in Africa and 9 per cent in the USSR. North American waters contributed a small proportion because of low productivity and pollution. The steady growth of fresh-water fish production is mainly attributable to the expansion of traditional catches from rivers and flood plains to newly created man-made lakes especially in Africa. Another contributory factor is the intensive pond culture in China and parts of South-East Asia.

Marine fisheries' landings amounted to 74.6 million tons in 1983. On account of the distribution and productivity of coastal zones, one half of this catch was concentrated in the North-East Atlantic and North-West Pacific. At present, only 70 per cent of the world catch is used for direct consumption while the rest is taken up for production of fish meal and oil. Statistics show that marine landings have increased by one million tons per year over the past few years. This growth rate could be maintained to the end of the century, when a catch around 100 metric tons should be possible. A projected demand of 140 metric tons for the year 2000 and beyond far exceeds what the ocean systems, as we know them today, can supply.

Future Trends: with regard to fresh-water fisheries, there are indications that most of the fish stocks in man-made African lakes are fully exploited, except for certain swamp areas in Botswana and Sudan. Overfishing, particularly with commercial trawlers, has caused serious damage in several large lakes. In Asia, although reservoir development has increased fresh-water catches, some losses in production have been recorded mainly owing to more intensive husbandry and increasing use of pesticides. Over-enrichment and pollution have remained the principal causes of damage to European fresh water fisheries. Of the 11 migratory species of fish that formerly occurred in the Rhine, for example, nine had virtually disappeared by 1978 and practically no commercially useful fisheries remained. On the other hand, because of pollution control measures, some of the migratory fishes have returned to the Thames. Although annual catch rates for marine fisheries have been increasing, the share of traditional varieties has been steadily decreasing. The increases have been accounted for by mackerel, squid, capelin and whiting, all till recently considered non-traditional. This decline of the traditional fishery is attributed mainly to overfishing especially in the Atlantic and some parts of the Pacific. The World Conservation Strategy has argued that had stocks not been damaged by overfishing, world yields in 1980 would have been 10 to 20 million tons more than what they were.[22] To a large extent, current yields have been maintained by the development of traditional varieties.

Yields from aquaculture represent about 10 per cent of world production of fishery products. Thus they have doubled during the last decade. Prospects are encouraging in this field. Global yields are increasing. Intensive culture of high-unit-value species, such as pen-rearing of salmon and culture of shrimp, is approaching the point of economic feasibility, and the extensive culture of animals that utilize very short food chains— oysters, mussels, mullet—has the potential for enormous expansion with existing technology.

A five- to ten-fold increase is projected by the year 2000 provided the necessary scientific, financial and organizational support is available.

Countries such as Norway and Scotland have found this an effective way of resource utilization. Aquaculture is comparatively economic, as it requires few inputs. An added advantage is that aquaculture can be carried out at all commercial levels— individual, family, co-operative or large business. It therefore provides a viable solution to developing countries' food and job security and can utilize otherwise unemployed or underemployed labour efficiently.

However, while industrialized countries will continue to develop energy-intensive and high technology culture species that require high-protein diets, the substantial production of herbivorous species in natural waters, designed to yield relatively low-cost animal protein, should expand even more rapidly. This will be particularly important for developing countries in tropical and subtropical areas with year-round growing seasons. But science will have to improve the technology required for extensive culture-production of inexpensive animal protein by such methods as genetic selection for high food-conversion efficiency and rapid growth, testing of low-cost diets from natural products and training of technicians. International co-operation and national institutes will have a lead role in this.

Aquaculture offers options for small-scale, low-technology and labour-intensive operations in developing countries. Aquaculture has a future role to play in food security and rural development, generally, through the provision of a better diet, jobs and a cash crop. Expansion of food production through aquaculture must be a matter of national policy and national priority.

In the process of developing inland fisheries and aquaculture, developing countries will have to protect the interests of the landless poor. This will call for well-planned programmes of resettlement and re-employment, derived from the people's own stated preferences.

Restoring The Land

Desertification*

The World Desertification Map identifies 29 per cent of the earth's land area as subject to varying degrees of desertification—slight, moderate or severe. An additional 6 per cent is classified as extremely severe. The process of desertification affects every region of the globe—Australia, China and Mongolia, Mediterranean Africa, Mediterranean Europe, Mexico, North America, South America, South and West Asia, sub-Saharan Africa and the USSR. However, it is more menacing in the drylands of South America, Asia and Africa where 18.5 per cent (870 million ha.) of all productive lands is severely desertified. Figure 3 indicates trends of desertification (see page 68).

The large populations supported by these lands further illustrate the significance of the problem. In 1984, 850 million people were reported to be living in drylands, of whom 500

---

* Desertification is defined as largely man-made processes which can destroy or diminish the biological potential of land.

Figure 3

CATEGORIES AND MAJOR NATURAL RESOURCES

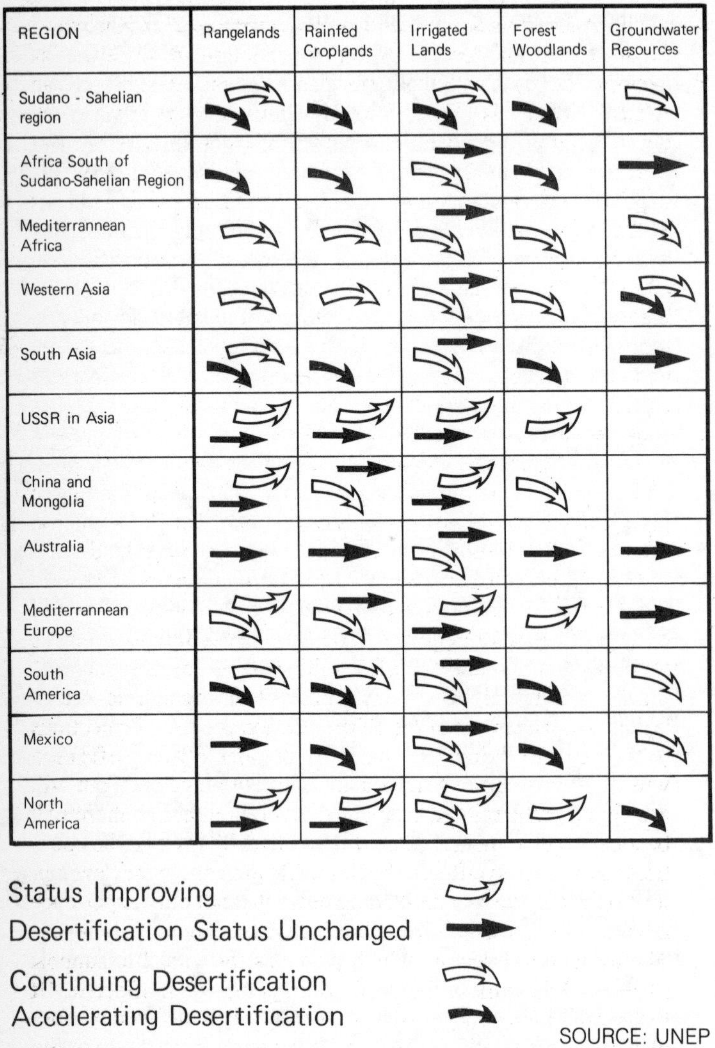

REGION	Rangelands	Rainfed Croplands	Irrigated Lands	Forest Woodlands	Groundwater Resources
Sudano - Sahelian region					
Africa South of Sudano-Sahelian Region					
Mediterrannean Africa					
Western Asia					
South Asia					
USSR in Asia					
China and Mongolia					
Australia					
Mediterrannean Europe					
South America					
Mexico					
North America					

Status Improving

Desertification Status Unchanged

Continuing Desertification

Accelerating Desertification

SOURCE: UNEP

million comprised the rural component. Of these, 230 million were on lands affected by severe desertification. Twenty per cent of the population on irrigated lands is moderately affected, while 15 per cent is severely struck by desertification.

The mass media have recently drawn the attention of the world to the extent of desertification-derived human suffering as exemplified by the Sahelian-Sudano region of sub-Saharan Africa. What is little known, however, is that such desertification-related human suffering on a small scale has occurred throughout history. What is now important is that man's knowledge and understanding of the underlying causes of this phenomenon have increased considerably. We are now better equipped both to minimize the spread of desertification and to restore the lands on which it has occurred. The global nature of desertification is also better appreciated not only in terms of its distribution but also in terms of its shared causes and consequences. Among the consequences that are of most concern to the international community and neighbouring countries, even those not directly affected, are: loss of genetic resources, hydrological disruption, increase of atmospheric dust, and loss of production and markets. In 1983, annual losses in production due to desertification were estimated at US$26 billion of which $7.4 billion represented desertified rangelands.

The prospects to the year 2000 and beyond are not encouraging. On the contrary, they are frightening. Land lost as a result of desertification or degraded to desert-like conditions continues to grow at an annual rate of 6 million ha. And each year, 21 million additional ha. of land provide no economic return because of the spread of the desertification process. Projections to the year 2000 indicate that present rates of desertification will be maintained in irrigated areas and in rangelands but will accelerate in the rainfed croplands. Overall, although there will be local improvements, gains will be offset by losses. The countries most severely affected by desertification are in the developing countries, the worst hit being those that not only experience adverse climatic conditions, but are also economically weak. The agricultural sector, which provides the vital life-support systems of the bulk of the population, is the worst affected. Of the developing countries' drylands, the Sahelian-Sudano zones of Africa, and to a lesser extent those countries to their south,

Figure 4

RURAL POPULATION AFFECTED BY MODERATE OR SEVERE DESERTIFICATION RESPECTIVELY IN THE MAJOR REGIONS AND SUBREGIONS OF THE DRYLANDS UNDER THE MAIN TYPES OF LAND USE. (MILLIONS) .

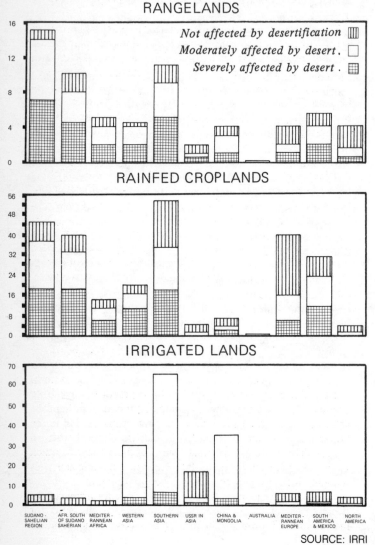

SOURCE: IRRI

are low-income countries with unfavourable climatic regimes. They therefore suffer most from desertification. In their arid and semi-arid lands are to be found 80 per cent of the moderately affected and 85 per cent of the severely hit people, as Figure 4 shows.

The causes of desertification include drought, rapid rates of growth of both human and animal populations and detrimental land-use practices (especially deforestation). Adverse terms of trade and civil strife also contribute to accelerate desertification. Deserts are the results of natural processes, but what cannot be denied is that humanity accelerates the process, contributing to desertification, both through its activities and its policies.

The impact of sustained drought on the world's drylands, notably in Africa, has drastically reduced food production. Sustained drought leads not only to the loss of natural vegetation, it also prevents farmers and pastoralists from re-establishing the necessary protective cover. A process of desertification thus begins, which is difficult to arrest and reverse unless *inter alia* favourable periods of rainfall occur.

The second underlying cause of desertification is population growth. Although most developing countries have recorded increases in rural populations, the most dramatic rates of growth have taken place in the Sahelian-Sudano region. Human population increases, however, have been surpassed by those of livestock. For example, the number of small livestock in the Sahelian rangelands is already greater than in the pre-drought years of the late 1960s, especially in the Horn of Africa. As a result, there is increased pressure on these already fragile ecosystems, the low carrying-capacity of which becomes further over-burdened. The final result is the collapse of the system.

The effects of inappropriate land-use practices have been exacerbated by the development policies pursued in most of the affected countries. A preference for cash crops has led to the utilization of unsuitable rangelands and has forced herdsmen to rear their cattle on marginal lands. In the pursuit of quick gains, urban entrepreneurs have engaged in economic activities without sufficient appreciation of the environment.

The unfavourable international terms of trade for primary products have reinforced government-engineered pressure for increasing cash-crop production at any cost. Producers are expected to grow more cash crops and, as they and their nations get poorer and fall into deeper debt, they overexploit the fragile ecological base to maximize their incomes and foreign exchange.

Not the least in importance is the civil strife which many of the worst affected countries have experienced over the last decade or so. Not only have these wars diverted investments from essential developmental and rehabilitation projects, but they have created an enormous number of refugees who, by applying untold pressure on the land, both contribute to the desertification process and hamper measures to arrest it.

The Plan Of Action To Combat Desertification.
The world became concerned with the problems of desertification when drought hit the Sahel in the period 1968-73. The world's concern culminated in the 1977 United Nations Conference on Desertification. This Conference drew up a Plan of Action to Combat Desertification in which UNEP was assigned the co-ordinating role. A discussion on what is to be done as a response to desertification must clearly start by looking at this global plan. Can desertification be arrested, lands restored and food security in the affected areas achieved through the Plan and similar strategies? Despite the existence of the Plan, desertification continues, apparently unabated, and ecological rehabilitation is far from being realized. Indeed, the indications are that desertification has intensified since 1977. As shown in Table 8 the numbers affected have grown and are growing. The problem gets worse.

1. an enhancement of worldwide awareness of and concern over desertification problems;
2. the stimulation of research in relevant areas such as long-term weather forecasting, remote-sensing applications, climatic modelling, water conservation, plant breeding for drought and salt resistance and the impact of social factors on the desertification process;
3. the conducting of training programmes in afforestation, sand-dune stabilization and range management. The number of persons trained has, however, been relatively insignificant; and
4. the initiation of afforestation and sand-dune stabilization

activities at both local and national levels. The most effective of these have been those that have been organized and implemented at the local level. Success has therefore been somewhat limited in scale.

Table 8 : Human Numbers Affected by Desertification

	(millions)		
	1977	1984	2000
Populations at risk of desertification	650	850	1200
Rural component	280	500	600
Severely affected	80	230	
Rural component of severely affected	57	135	

Source: Compiled from UNEP, General Assessment of Progress in the Implementation of the Plan of Action to Combat Desertification 1978-84. (Nairobi, 1984)

The Plan calls for the support and involvement of international and national institutions and local communities. Yet by 1984, of the $10 billion spent worldwide by bilateral and multilateral agencies on anti-desertification measures, only about one-tenth had been spent on the field control of desertification. In 1977, a programme to prevent further desertification was estimated to cost about $4.5 billion a year for a period of 20 years. The programme has received comparatively little financial support. It appears that investors shy away from activities such as those to combat desertification, since they do not yield short-term benefits.

At the national level, most governments seem unable to arrest desertification. In fact, many of them have not even developed national plans of action to combat desertification as proposed by the Plan. In addition, the responsibility for the control of desertification is shared by many ministries and is often un-coordinated.

The regional nature of the problem has been accepted by many governments and some regional organizations have been established in response. These include the Permanent Interstate

Committee on Drought Control in the Sahel (CILSS). However, even CILSS remains ineffective because of political squabbling and the shortage of qualified staff. Its field record leaves much to be desired.

People's participation at the grass roots level still remains largely untapped. Where they have been reached, their needs have not been clearly articulated into efforts to combat desertification. At the same time, they have not been made aware of the broader macroprocesses and effects of desertification. This underlines the special importance of establishing government policies that provide appropriate mechanisms, incentives and education programmes to ensure the acceptance and implementation of measures at community level. People's participation through consultation will in turn ensure that proposed measures are appropriate to local ecosystems and existing social organizations.

The international community should readdress the problem and focus more on causes and sources instead of merely responding to the effects. There should be a two-pronged approach. In addition to arresting desertification in the most seriously affected areas, greater attention should be paid to those areas that are in danger of desertification and to areas classified as being only slightly to very moderately desertified. The strategies and programmes to forestall and/or arrest the desertification process in these latter areas should be adopted at the international, regional and national levels.

National governments should give priority to establishing national programmes to combat desertification and to creating or augmenting national machineries for implementing such programmes. Where these already exist, they should be better coordinated and better designed to act in the field. People's participation should be encouraged so that the programmes formulated are in harmony with existing social, cultural and ecological systems. The role of NGOs in implementing action-oriented projects should be acknowledged and encouraged.

Population

As the global family of peoples doubles yet again in the next

40 years, the world will possess an unprecedented pool of potential knowledge, creativity, understanding and happiness or misery and despair. In meeting the challenge of food security to the year 2000 and beyond, we have stressed the overriding need to release this potential and transform it into a healthy and productive resource. Of all the resources needed in the future a healthy, well-trained and educated people is the most precious.

Releasing this potential has rarely been easy; focusing it on essential tasks is even more difficult. In the preceding discussion, we have stressed a few essential strategies aimed at sustainable increases in food production. They include, first and foremost, improving the access of people to the skills, resources, livelihoods and income they need both to achieve sustainable increases in production and to command their share of the food produced. We have also highlighted many of the constraints that prevent the co-ordinated pursuit of these strategies and suggested several new policy directions to overcome them.

In a number of countries, including some in Africa, West Asia and Latin America, the population problem is not that there are too many people for the resource base, but that population growth and migration rates appear greatly to outstrip present and future prospects for developing the capacity to produce more food. In many other countries, especially in Asia, the problem is that there are too many people for the resource base to support at present and projected levels of technology. In most developing countries, a substantial reduction in projected rates of population growth and in the ultimate level at which the population stabilizes would significantly improve their chances for food security.

At the beginning of this century, the world's family numbered 1.7 billion people. Almost as many, 1.6 billion, will be added in the 5000 days remaining to the end of this century. Of this increase, about 56 per cent will occur in Asia, 25 per cent in Africa and 11 per cent in Latin America. Industrialized countries as a group will grow by 8 per cent.

These rates are projected to continue well into the next century. Asia could double its 1980 population to 5.0 billion before stabilizing; Latin America could triple from 360 million to 1.2 billion and, as shown in Table 9 below, Africa is projected to increase its population six times before it stabilizes.

Table 9 : African Population Projections, 1980-2100

Selected Countries	1950	1980	2000	2025	2050	2100	Total Fertility Rate, 1983	Year in Which NRR* =1
Cameroon	4.6	8.7	17	30	42	50	6.5	2030
Ethiopia	18.0	37.7	64	106	142	173	5.5	2035
Ghana	4.4	11.5	23	40	53	62	7.0	2025
Kenya	5.8	16.6	37	69	97	116	8.0	2030
Malawi	2.9	6.0	11	21	29	36	7.6	2040
Mozambique	6.5	12.1	22	39	54	67	6.5	2035
Niger	2.9	5.5	11	20	29	38	7.0	2040
Nigeria	40.6	84.7	163	295	412	509	6.9	2035
Tanzania	7.8	18.8	37	69	96	120	7.0	2035
Uganda	4.8	12.6	25	46	64	80	7.0	2035
Zaire	14.2	27.1	50	86	116	139	6.3	2030
Other Sub-Sahara	59.8	121.7	218	381	524	651	6.5	2040
Total Sub-Sahara	172.4	363.0	678	1,202	1,658	2,041	6.7	2040
Total Other Africa	42.6	89.6	148	225	282	319	5.5	2025
Total Africa	215.0	452.6	826	1,427	1,940	2,360	6.5	2040

Notes: * NRR refers to net reproduction rate. When NRR = 1, fertility is at replacement level

Source: R. McNamara: *The Challenges for Sub-Saharan Africa (Sir John Crawford Memorial Lecture, Washington D.C., 1985)*

What do these rapid rates of growth mean for food security and development? The answer varies greatly for different countries and regions, but some consequences are clear. Take employment and livelihoods, for example. We can estimate the size of the workforce now because its numbers are already with us. There is only a 15-year time lag before the average newborn child becomes a worker. By the turn of the century, developing countries will add some 780 million additional workers to the 1980 figure of 1.25 billion, at rates of 30 to 40 million a year. As a group, they will have to create as many new jobs and livelihoods in the next 25 years as they have created up to this point in history.

We have stressed that sustainable paths to food security can be a source of millions of livelihoods a year in rural areas—*if* the young have access to the education and skills needed to benefit from new technologies and vastly expanded extension services. While some developing countries have achieved near miracles in improving the nutrition, health and education of their citizens, these projected *rates* of increase constitute almost impossible barriers to future gains. In sub-Saharan Africa, for example, the poorest region of the world with the highest rates of population growth (an average of 6.7 children per woman in 1983), most countries will see their school age population double in the next 15 years and triple or quadruple in the next 40.

We have referred to the many assessments which establish that the availability of natural resources poses no fundamental constraint on future food security, at least on a global basis. But these assessments are meaningful only if it is possible to project a steady improvement in the quality of the human resources applied to their development. Of 40 sub-Saharan countries (excluding Djibouti and the smaller island nations), for example, 14 do not have enough land, water and forests—assuming subsistence-level farming—to support their present populations on a sustainable basis. They account for one-third of the land area of sub-Saharan Africa and about half of its 1981 population. Whatever paths these countries choose, their only hope is the rapid development of their human resources and through them access to higher levels of technology and development. The same is true of the land-abundant countries referred to earlier which occupy about 30 per cent of the region's land, but account for only one-fifth of its 1981 population.

Runaway population growth, then, may result in reduced access to education, health and nutrition, the essential ingredients of human-resource development and of sustainable paths to food security. Indeed, mounting unemployment, marginalization and poverty may aggravate pressures on the ecological base. Access to safe water and new wood growth may become even more difficult as human numbers increase, adding to deforestation, soil erosion and desertification and reinforcing the downward spiral of economic decline, social instability, misery and despair.

Fortunately, the national and regional rates of population growth and ultimate levels of stabilization cited above are not predetermined.

Table 10 : Population Growth Rates, by Region, 1950-85
(annual average in per cent)

Region	1950-55	1960-65	1970-75	1975-80	1980-85
Africa	2.11	2.44	2.74	3.00	3.01
Latin America	2.72	2.80	2.51	2.37	2.30
East Asia*	2.08	1.81	2.36	1.47	1.20
South Asia	2.00	2.51	2.44	2.30	2.20
All Developing Countries	2.11	2.30	2.46	2.14	2.02

Notes: Excluding Japan
Source: United Nations 1982 assessment

Beginning in the early 1970s, a slow deceleration in population growth became evident in all regions of the developing world except Africa. No other nation matches the Chinese in their efforts to limit their numbers, but others have been quite successful, notably Sri Lanka, India, Mexico, etc. in reducing their growth rates.

Even in sub-Saharan Africa attitudes are beginning to change. In 1984, 36 countries adopted the Kilimanjaro Programme of Action on population, which recognized that access to nutrition, health and education services, especially for women, was fundamental to family planning. At the grassroots level attitudinal changes have been noted, particularly among rural women. Not so long ago, many poor women in Africa wished to have more daughters to help them fetch water and wood and sons to see to their needs in old age. Now, an impressive number sees that as the land degrades, they face greater hardships in bringing up children. It is not our task to advise the Commission on the elements of birth control programmes. It is our duty, however, to stress the crucial importance of giving higher priority to such programmes in all countries as a part of an integrated attack on the food security challenge.

The other part of the population/food equation is, of course, the possibility of increasing the supply of food while rates of population growth are contained. In this regard, thought should be given to the introduction, wherever feasible, of new technologies in agricultural production even in the most underdeveloped economies. And this, precisely, because the introduction of such technologies may well be the only means of ensuring the increased food supplies for which there will be such dire need. We wish to draw attention, therefore, to the importance of research in genetic engineering, to the possibility through these new technologies of producing plants and groups of plants that have a greater resilience and an improved resistance to environmental and climatic stresses and to the possibility of controlled environment agriculture. Indeed, the use of controlled environmental technologies is already more widespread in China than in any other country in the world.

There are more mundane methods that can, in addition, be more generally employed. For example, the utilization of multiple cropping practices may assist in coping with rising populations. In Asia, where the proportion of potential land under cultivation was 78 per cent in 1975, about 7.5 per cent of the cultivated land is cropped more than once. In some countries the proportion is much greater, reaching as high as 52 per cent. In sub-Saharan Africa, where the system is little practised, there is much scope for its adoption.

We are convinced that if everything works well, as population growth rates continue to fall, as the world gets its policies right, and as new technologies in agriculture are introduced at the appropriate time, the misery and despair, which now seem almost inevitable, will be avoided.

Reorienting Agricultural Policy

Global Thinking, National And Regional Action

If the food security challenge is to be met for the year 2000 and beyond, with production rising at rates of 3 to 4 per cent annually, it will be necessary to marshal and utilize the human and natural resource potential in the most effective and efficient way possible. The experience of the past several decades demonstrates clearly that this requires more than ''good'' programmes. Well-funded and well-managed irrigation, transport, storage and other infrastructure projects; well-conceived soil and water conservation projects; integrated forest management projects; etc. are not enough. Whether in developed or developing countries, such programmes can be, and usually are, over-ridden and undermined by inappropriate agricultural, economic, trade and other policies. These policies are now "ecologically blind" in their conception, funding and implementation. They must be given "ecological eyes". One critical issue for food security to the year 2000 and beyond is how best to achieve this, locally, nationally and internationally.

The issue includes (but goes well beyond) the traditional question of adding on the environmental dimension of programmes and projects in order to capture and internalize what economists fondly call "externalities". It is, of course, critically important that this be done. All agricultural activities, including farming, affect the environment positively or negatively. If the effects are negative, they will take the form of costs once the assimilative capacity of the environment in question has been exceeded. These costs present two problems: first, their evaluation is extremely difficult; second, the health, property or environment damaged is often not priced, at least not in a market, and deducing a price for it is usually difficult and always controversial.

However controversial, these costs cannot be avoided; one way or another, they will be paid: but by whom? when? and how? They can be paid in the form of damage to health (in the case of workers' exposure to pesticides); damage to property (in the case of reduced output through degradation of land as the result of practices that cause erosion, salinization and acidification), or damage to the environment held in common (in the case of phosphate or nitrate pollution of waters resulting from over-use of chemicals). When a community's tolerance to that form of damage is exceeded, governments may intervene, and often do, transferring the costs elsewhere. This may be to the private sector, by requiring various add-on measures to alleviate or stop the damage, the costs being passed on through reduced profits or increased prices. In the case of agriculture, however, the costs are more often transferred to the public sector and paid for through various forms of taxes.

Contrary to the popular view, environmental costs can be huge. If not planned for, they can completely undermine a major investment. This has too often been the case with, for example, major dam projects where a large population has been displaced and impoverished and where the failure to control land use in the watershed has resulted in rapid siltation of the reservoir; or with irrigation projects, where the failure to build in drainage has resulted in salinization and abandonment of land. The social and political as well as the economic costs of lost production from soil acidification in Europe could become catastrophic within the next two decades.

Some people are of the opinion that concern for protecting the environmental and resource base for agriculture is a luxury that the "poor agricultural sector" in all societies, and especially in developing countries, cannot afford. These views are based on a misunderstanding of the issues. If a country wishes to pay attention to the economic costs (and benefits) of agricultural production—and all countries do—it must deal with the environmental costs. Taking the costs of protecting and sustaining the resource bases of an agricultural programme into the decision calculus is no more "in conflict" with development than is taking in the costs of seeds, fertilizers or energy. The environmental costs may be high—and with programmes of investment, infrastructure, input subsidies and price supports growing steadily in scale, today they are often very high. This notwithstanding, even the strongest advocates of development must take costs into account if their true concern is to advance the national welfare. If they do not, the development objectives of the investment, which cannot be divorced from the environmental objectives, will not be achieved.

It is important to take the environmental costs of agricultural programmes and projects into the decision calculus without making invidious distinctions between environment and development. But it is not enough. Even if that were done, the political, economic, social and ecological goals of the programme could be completely undermined by inappropriate agricultural policies.

Investment in research and linked farm-extension programmes, for example, must be increased several-fold in developing countries if their land, productivity and human potential are to be realized. However, the goals behind such investment can be weakened or undermined completely if the questions of location, manning and, more important, priorities for research, are conceived on a national or, worse, international scale and if the environmental and socio-economic heterogeneity of the target areas are ignored. This has been too often the case to date, with an inevitable mismatching of agricultural development and the needs and potentials of individual localities. The effect has been to create a coarse-grained agriculture, manifest in a large-scale uniformity of crop varieties and techniques of cultivation. The issue is not merely one of quantity and investment but quality and method. Agricultural research has to be oriented towards the more complex and diverse systems of resource-poor farmers as opposed to the more uniform and simpler farming systems of resource-rich farmers.

These problems are now being recognized. The persistent gap in yield between agricultural research stations and farmers' fields, produced by differences in both environmental and socio-economic conditions, is receiving attention. The evidence of pest-resistance to chemicals and of deteriorating land and declining yields following intensive cultivation of high-yielding varieties has registered.

Policies governing the location and financing of land development and irrigation schemes, of agro-processing facilities, of colonization schemes and the establishment of marketing networks also need to be given an ecological dimension. Distortions in tax, incentive and subsidy policies that encourage practices detrimental to the resource base of agriculture are well documented in both developed and developing countries and must be changed.

In developing countries, the poverty of support systems leaves small and subsistence farmers reluctant to assume the risks associated with new seeds and productivity packages and leaves agriculture without the essential support that it needs. In developed market economies, the problem is over-rich incentive programmes that penalize the resource base in pursuit of short-term gains in productivity.

Large numbers of farmers and their spokesmen are becoming concerned about the impact of subsidy-driven practices on the quality of the land they pass on to their children. Yet the pressure to increase production at the cost of the resource base will remain as long as it is in the short-term economic interest of farmers to do so, and as long as the policy structure within which they operate reinforces and does not correct their necessarily short-term arithmetic.

A redesigning of these policies is essential to the goals of sustainable agriculture. Moreover, such a revision can serve not only to improve the resource base, and enable sustainable future gains in productivity, but also to reduce significantly existing levels of public expenditure on agricultural subsidies. This should be a welcome prospect in these critical times of high budget deficits.

Obviously, no quick solution is possible; no one set of answers that will shift patterns of production and trade overnight is conceivable. But there can be a clear plan to reverse what is so evidently a wrong direction and to move gradually toward proper adjustments.

Only national governments and people can take the fundamental actions needed to realize their own food security potential. But today, no national government can do this on its own. That will be even more true tomorrow as the forces of economic, ecological and political interdependence erode further the reality of sovereignty and independence.

Some developing countries in Asia, such as India and China, have or are rapidly gaining the infrastructure or experience needed to move in these directions themselves and to provide support to other developing countries wishing to do the same. However, greater support, taking a lead role in certain specific spheres, must be provided mainly by the industrialized countries.

Strengthening the environmental and developmental foundations of food security from a global point of view, requires a series of steps that will, among other things, reduce incentives that inevitably cause over-production and non-competitive production in developed market economies, but do the opposite in developing countries. The discussion below will suggest some directions that should be followed: increase capital for land development in Latin America and Africa and apply yield-increasing technologies in all developing countries, increase infrastructure, strengthen research capacity and linked extension services, induce land reform and improve and enrich incentive systems.

This will require a difficult shift to thinking globally about an industry that has become global. Trade in agricultural products tripled between 1950 and 1970 and has doubled since then.

Yet, when it comes to farming, countries are at their most conservative, continuing to think in strictly local or, at best, national terms and concerned, above all, to protect their own farmers at the expense of competitors. The recognition of a common interest in orderly trading patterns, always weak, has now almost disappeared under the pressure of contradictory policies.

There are some positive signs of change, but they are few in number and still overshadowed by forces that would maintain the momentum of existing processes. A start has been made by the World Bank and by some multilateral and bilateral development assistance agencies working through the Development Assistance Committee (DAC)/Environment Committee of OECD, for example. They have begun to re-examine their policies to ensure that they do not continue to support projects that are non-sustainable and that result in reducing rather than increasing the economic prospects of the receiving country. But these examinations of policies have been conducted at a very low level and very few concrete changes can be identified. The top political and administrative leadership of these agencies must become personally engaged to carry through the necessary reforms.

Beyond that, countries must move towards more open trade policies, recognizing that all parties lose through protectionist policies, which reduce trade in food products that represent genuine comparative advantage. And they must begin by redesigning their trade, tax and incentive systems against criteria that include ecological as well as economic sustainability and genuine international comparative advantage.

Towards New Agricultural Systems

Government intervention in agriculture is the rule in both developed and developing countries and it is here to stay.

Public investment in agricultural infrastructure is universal: water development, dams and reservoirs, large- and small-scale irrigation, roads, rail and river transport, storage facilities, rural education, etc. The existence of this infrastructure, along with agricultural research institutes and colleges linked to extension services bringing technical and other information to the farm, assisted farm credit and marketing services and a range of other support systems can take much of the credit for the successes of the last half century. The weakness of agriculture in much of Africa, Latin America and some other developing countries stems in large part from the weakness of these systems.

Intervention has taken other forms as well. The management of virtually the entire food cycle—inputs and outputs, domestic sales, exports, public procurement, storage and distribution, price controls and subsidies—has been common practice in most countries. So have various forms of regulation of land use, acreage, crop variety, etc.

Some of these interventions are part of a long-term strategy to build up the productive base of agriculture. Others, particularly those involving tax relief, direct subsidies and price controls, are the result of annual responses to short-term pressures.

There is no doubt that the huge production gains achieved in North America, Western Europe and other developed market economies reflect, in large part, the rich incentive systems that have been introduced since World War II. In recent years, however, these systems have lost whatever coherence they may have had. They are now studded with contradictions and anomalies that encourage the degradation of the agricultural resource base and, in the longer run, are a cause of more harm than help to the agricultural industry.

In developing countries, the resource base is under sustained attack, but the causes are different. The major tasks of providing infrastructure-support systems are incomplete as also, in many countries, are measures to carry through needed land reform and to improve equity and access. These gaps together with incentive systems that are always underfinanced and sometimes misdirected, reinforce poverty and poverty-derived pressures on the agricultural resource base.

Developing Countries: sustainable agriculture and food security in developing countries, especially in Africa and Latin America, demands a policy of action on a number of fronts: technical, developmental, social and political, as well as greatly improved and enriched incentive systems.

Subsistence requirements often force farmers to grow foodgrain even when it is not optimal. Small farm size results in many "externalities", from farm practices that induce erosion and from the use of pesticides. Major gaps in infrastructure and support systems make it difficult for farmers to switch to more optimal cropping patterns, while unsolved problems of land tenure and land distribution lead to the marginalization of small-holders and to improper land use.

Market interventions in developing countries are often in-effective for lack of an organizational structure for procurement and distribution. Farmers are exposed to a high degree of uncer-tainty, and price support systems have often favoured the urban dweller or are limited to a few commercially oriented crops, leading to distortions of cropping patterns that add to destructive pressures on the resource base.

In many cases, trade policies are slanted against food security. Developing countries are net food exporters in the wide sense. Certain items such as beef and fish go to feed the very people in developed countries on whom they depend for their grain. In 1982, food imports by developing countries totalled $52 billion against their exports of $60 billion. Third World countries and regions must reappraise their policies on international food trade and address the contradictions they create. It may well be sensible for some countries to export some forms of food and import others, provided that in this process they are able to protect the interests of poor producers and consumers.

Planned Economy Countries: some agricultural policies, parti-cularly those pertaining to access and control of the factors of production—land, inputs, technology and labour organization—have led to increased yields in some smaller countries. In the majority of cases, however, other aspects of labour organization have had adverse effects on production, contrary to what had been expected. Relaxation of some of these aspects has proved advantageous to national output in those countries that have tried it.

While the subsidy incentive to individual farmers, most marked in developed market economies, is absent here, fertilizer consumption, like that of other chemicals, has been increasing quite impressively. Indeed, the annual rate of change has been higher than in the market economy countries. The disastrous effects on the soils and ground-water aquifers are equally alarm-ing, while damage to surface water is threatening the water-based ecosystems. Clearly, planners will have to evolve policies which, while moving nearer to the goals of self-reliance in food, do not damage the agricultural resource base or human health.

Meanwhile, greater efforts will have to go into reclaiming the land from acidification and pursuing irrigation systems that will avoid or at least minimize the risks of salinization and alkalization.

Developed Market Economies: the incentive systems found today in most developed market economies have become extremely expensive, thus imposing a heavy and annually increasing burden on the budgets and debt load of the countries concerned. For example, in 1983, it was estimated that in the United Kingdom direct Exchequer support to farmers and the effects of the Common Agricultural Policy (CAP), including the impact on consumer prices, amounted to a subsidy of approximately 20,000 per farmer.

While the systems vary greatly, virtually the entire food cycle now attracts direct or indirect subsidies: inputs (such as assisted loans, interest on capital, O & M, chemicals, etc), outputs, (through price support for many products), storage and domestic sales. These have led to large and unmanageable surpluses, and it has become politically more attractive, and often cheaper, to ship surpluses than to store them. Indeed, there are some political leaders in the European Community, for example, who have seen it as their duty to Third World countries to create surpluses for export. Yet, these heavily subsidized surpluses have depressed prices of commodities such as sugar in countries in which agriculture is the mainstay of their economies. Yet the pressure to export continues to grow to such an extent that exports have now come to attract subsidies, thus raising the prospect of a destabilizing trade war in agricultural products.

Food aid, too, because it is assumed to combine morality with political necessity, has acquired great appeal as a means of reducing surpluses. There is no doubt that food aid is essential to ease hunger in an emergency situation. It does little, however, to prevent starvation after the emergency has ended. Moreover, in normal situations, the growing volume of food aid only compounds the real problems in receiving countries by reducing the pressure for policy change to stimulate local production and relieve destructive poverty-induced pressures on the resource base. Coupled with low-priced imports, food aid depresses prices paid to local farmers and makes it easier for governments to relax in their efforts to develop agricultural infrastructures.

The ecological consequences of a heavily subsidized production system are also becoming evident. They vary from region to region, but include lower productivity on previously good-quality soils, as the result of intensive production practices and/or over-use of chemicals, fertilizers and pesticides. They include the destruction of the countryside, clearing of hedgerows, parkbelts and other protective cover, levelling, occupation and cultivation of marginal land and watershed protection areas. Moreover, the nitrate pollution of ground-water aquifers has become a serious problem in many areas due to the over-use of nitrate fertilizers, which often qualify for subsidies.

During the great export boom of the 1960s and 1970s, prices soared and advice from government officials and agricultural experts in countries such as Canada and the US as well as Western Europe, reinforced policies that encouraged farmers to bring more land into production. The landscape was transformed. Several million hectares of marginal land were brought under the plough, as farmers were encouraged by measures such as tax relief for land development, crop support loans and cash subsidies. Attempts by soil conservation services and volunteer groups to control land conversion through small-grant programmes, acquisition of special areas and persuasion were powerless in the face of tax, economic and agricultural subsidies that encourage conversion.

The financial, economic and ecological effects of current incentive systems are beginning to be questioned by many governments and groups, including farm organizations themselves. While these systems may not be removed for the time being, it is clearly in the interests of all concerned, in particular the agricultural industry itself, that they be changed. Their financial and economic burden has to be reduced. The negative impact of unwanted surpluses on the economic and resource base of developing countries' agriculture has to be eliminated. Most important is that their ecological contradictions are removed.

An agricultural policy for tomorrow: each nation should examine carefully the criteria that now prevail for:

1. the reform of the land ownership tenure system;

2. agricultural research and extension systems;
3. credit and input supply systems;
4. the provision of public irrigation and land development;
5. land colonization and resettlement schemes;
6. the location of agro-processing facilities;
7. the establishment of marketing networks;
8. incentives such as entitlement to tax deductions, accelerated depreciation and assisted loans for land development, direct subsidies for inputs, outputs and storage;
9. rural roads, electrification and infrastructure.

Under most systems today, these criteria are "ecologically blind". Accepting that agricultural policy must serve a range of interdependent political, economic *and*, in the future, ecological goals, these criteria must be modified. They should be augmented by some new sustainability criteria designed both to discourage farm practices that reduce the quality of the environment and encourage practices that at least maintain and preferably enhance the quality of the land and its associated forests and waters. Agricultural policy tends to operate within a national framework with uniform prices and subsidies, standardized norms for the provision of support services, indiscriminate financing of infrastructure investments, etc. What is needed is a measure of regional differentiation so that the farmers' response in each ecological region is appropriate to what is sustainable in that region.

Sustainability criteria will require that agricultural policy takes into account the "best use" of the land. This will need the identification of lands or areas qualifying for different types of public investment, support services, promotional measures, regulatory restrictions, fiscal subsidies and other incentives and disincentives, and devising modifications to existing systems and financing. While many considerations will be unique to each local and national situation, it is possible to set out a number of general criteria and guidelines.

Identifying Lands: in identifying lands or areas of land that should or should not qualify for various forms of government intervention, at least three broad categories can be envisioned: the first is those lands (and associated vegetation and waters) with a significant potential for increased yields and productivity

89

on a sustained basis (enhancement areas); the second, those lands that are most at risk from existing agricultural and related forestry practices (prevention areas); the third, those lands whose productivity has been seriously reduced or even destroyed by past practices but where it is desirable or, perhaps, necessary to undertake restoration (restoration areas).

The means for identifying lands according to notions of "best use" are now available or can be made available. Most industrialized countries possess detailed inventories of their lands, forests and waters which describe surface and subsurface characteristics, soil quality and relationship to the watershed in which they are located. Most developing countries do not yet have such detailed inventories, but they can and should be constructed and at a much more rapid pace than heretofore. Indeed, improving the data base for agricultural planning at national, sub-national and local levels is one of the priority areas for action. If agricultural policy in developing countries is to have ecological eyes, accelerated programmes are mandatory for producing inventories of soil quality and land-use, mapping forests and waters, delineating watersheds, not to mention improving agro-meteorology and weather forecasting. Satellite monitoring and other rapidly evolving techniques should both reduce the time and cost needed for such programmes and greatly increase their usefulness.

The politics of selection could be facilitated by making it the special responsibility of a select board or commission, that would include outstanding representatives of the interests involved, particularly the poor and more marginalized segments of the population. The entire process must be essentially public in character with publicly agreed criteria. In particular, the criteria must combine "the best use" with the required levels of livelihood intensity.

Selection would have to involve considerations at more than one level, and range from the farm unit to the watershed. In some cases, the latter could and should require an international perspective. Examples abound of land use in one country having serious, and potentially disastrous, effects on the land and water resources of neighbouring countries. An international panel might be convened to advise on areas contiguous to national boundaries.

90

Enhancement Areas: lands or areas of land capable of sustaining intensive cropping and higher levels of livelihood intensity, and with a potential for increased yields and productivity, could benefit significantly from a fine-tuning of agricultural policy as could their associated vegetation and water resources. For example: in areas that are potentially subject to wind and water erosion, public intervention through subsidies and other measures should be oriented towards soil and water conservation practices.

For land located over recharge areas for underground aquifers that are subject to nitrate pollution, incentives might be introduced to induce farmers to adopt ecologically acceptable forms of maintaining soil fertility and increasing productivity.

In areas where pest resistance to chemicals has become, or will become, a problem, measures should be introduced to encourage the development and adoption of community-wide systems of integrated pest management.

With suitable programmes for forestry, horticulture or agroforestry development, wastelands can be rehabilitated, made more productive and capable of supporting more people.

At the farm, community or watershed level where the external costs of farm practices spill over onto neighbouring farms, communities, watersheds and even countries, it is entirely justified to orient agricultural policy, and especially to direct subsidies so that they are conditional upon the adoption of a plan for land and water saving and yield-inducing conservation practices. Inter-farm externalities are especially critical in areas with extremely small holdings, as found in many developing countries. Community co-operatives or other forms of shared responsibility could be encouraged for decisions affecting several producers, thereby providing properly designed and jointly administered agricultural policy.

Fine-tuning incentive systems will not be sufficient. Often they will have to be supplemented by direct regulation, including controls on acreage, cropping and inputs.

In most developing countries, other measures will also be required. Land reforms, (redistribution, consolidation of holdings, security of tenure) for example, are often a prerequisite to sustainable agriculture and could be pursued within the context of area-level plans with appropriate support and incentive systems.

The implementation of a watershed management plan for a hilly area provides an example of the range of intervention required. It may require a reorientation of cropping patterns to promote vegetation cover on steep slopes, fruit crops on middle slopes and terraced cultivation on gentler slopes. Among other things, such a transformation would require some form of land redistribution and consolidation to give each farmer a compact "workable holding" while compensating those whose land use would be severely restricted. It would require: a community co-operative or some other form of shared responsibility for pest, forest and water management; an assisted network for procurement, processing and distribution of the new crops to be produced; arrangements for the supply of seeds, saplings, agro-chemicals and other inputs, along with credit and insurance. More generally, transitional subsidies and incentive pricing will be required to promote the shift from subsistence cultivation of food grains and from felling of trees for fuel to the requirements of a watershed plan.

Prevention Areas: lands or areas of land and associated forests and waters that, by common consent, should not be developed for intensive agriculture (and, where developed, lands that should revert to other uses) would include:

1. lands needed to perform essential soil and water conservation functions in an intensively developed watershed (eg. uplands that support or should support forests);
2. marginal lands, such as grasslands and certain uplands and forests, whose development for intensive agriculture would accelerate erosion, loss of topsoil, siltation of lakes, rivers and reservoirs, desertification and climatic change;
3. wetlands vital to wildlife, flood control and water quality protection; and
4. bays and estuaries with present or potential use for aquaculture.

Lands so identified through participatory processes should be denied all forms of support and subsidy that would encourage their development for intensive agriculture, whether through bringing grasslands under the plough, felling upland forests or clearing designated wetlands and estuaries.

Such areas, on the other hand, might well support certain forms of use on an ecologically and economically sustainable basis: for example, grazing, fuelwood plantations, fruit farming, forestry, etc. Agricultural policy is seldom designed to encourage this. Indeed, a major problem with agricultural policy in both developed and developing countries is that it focuses attention on only a few crops and benefits only a minority of rural households. In some developing countries, food policy is sometimes designed with the interests of urban consumers only in mind and not those of rural producers. In redesigning systems, attention should be focused on a broader range of crops, including those that enhance grazing, soil and water conservation, etc.

Ecologically alert agricultural policies could help to convert hundreds of millions of the most erodable hectares to ecologically and economically appropriate uses. And they would do so more effectively and efficiently than any number of national or local soil and water conservation plans adopted with great fanfare but aborted at birth by powerful economic instruments that encourage farmers to do the exact opposite.

Restoration Areas: these would include lands or areas of land on which, because of past use, productivity has either been totally lost or has been so drastically reduced that yields are too low even to sustain farmers at subsistence level or to provide adequate returns on investment. They would also include lands from which the vegetative cover has been removed to such an extent that they are subject to degrees of accelerated erosion and water run-off, which reduce production on adjacent and downstream areas through, for example, the creation of flash floods and the siltation of rivers and reservoirs. They would also include areas that are so denuded that their mere presence leads to ''desertification creep'' and the loss of productivity in adjacent areas.

Whether particular areas should be restored or not would depend upon whether the benefits to be gained through restoration would exceed the costs of restoration including externalities. It is evident that restoration should not be undertaken unless a net gain is foreseen.

The type of treatment for areas to be restored would, of

course, vary with the site. Three generic methods, or combinations of these, are generally employed:

1. protection of the area in order to permit the natural regeneration of the vegetation;
2. the establishment of vegetation (trees, shrubs, grasses etc.) through planting; seeding etc.; and
3. the construction of bunds, terraces, etc.

Protection measures are often difficult to implement in areas in which there are large herds of animals or large numbers of people. It is in areas such as these, therefore, that the agreement and participation of the local people are of the highest importance. The State might also wish to declare such areas national reserves and to use its normal machinery to ensure that they remain protected. In such instances they would be treated as if they were forest reserves. Where these areas are privately held, the State might wish either to purchase the land from the owners or to provide incentives to them for its non-use.

Similar measures (the declaration of the areas as reserves or protected areas, the purchase of the lands or the provision of incentives) may be adopted in those restoration areas on which vegetation is to be planted, terraces to be constructed, etc.

Financing the Transition to Sustainable Agriculture and Food Security

National action: in the aggregate, an agricultural system based on criteria of sustainability should not require net subsidies. The income and tax-paying potential should be sufficient to finance the public investments and budgetary expenditures on special programmes, subsidies, etc. The real problem is that a regionally differentiated, ecologically oriented agricultural policy may constrain short and medium-term income potential in some areas and generate high earning in others. The basic approach should be to compensate those whose earnings are constrained in the interest of sustainability and raise the resources for this purpose by cutting back on unnecessary subsidies to those who are not so constrained. This will require a redirection of existing programmes. But, in Third World countries major investments will be required and the financing of these cannot come from such readjustments.

International Support: clearly, only national governments and peoples themselves can take the fundamental actions needed to reverse the steady deterioration of the resource base for agriculture that results from crippling distortions in the framework of economic and agricultural policy. No outside assistance, however massive, can possibly be a substitute for these essential national actions.

An increase in international assistance is, however, necessary and, given essential action by developing countries, can be effective. Financial institutions and multilateral and bilateral agencies should begin by systematically re-examining their current policies against the recommendations contained in this report. They should start to redirect those that now support programmes and projects that are non-sustainable.

The success of any strategy to put Third World agriculture on an ecologically and economically sustainable footing will continue to require external finance. The arguments for substantial—and increasing—levels of financial assistance are very powerful. Increasing assistance is needed to:

1. support the transitional requirements to long-term sustainable growth;
2. invest in the development of raw lands for agriculture in Africa and Latin America and in sustainable means of increasing yields and productivity;
3. invest in infrastructure needs, research institutes and extension services and human resource development;
4. arrest current trends in erosion, desertification, deforestation and degradation of the resource base for agriculture; and
5. promote knowledge of approaches with high sustainable livelihood intensity.

Unfortunately, such increases are not now in prospect. Indeed, on the basis of present plans, it appears possible that the flow of finance to developing countries could decline substantially below the totally inadequate levels of 1985.

In this regard, one thing is certain: financial assistance in the future should be provided only in support of policies, programmes and projects that add to the potential of the receiving country to create wealth on a sustainable basis. As demonstrated throughout this report, financial assistance has too often in the past supported policies, programmes, projects and commercial links that predictably resulted in consuming their own essential environmental and resource foundations and reducing the wealth and wealth-creating potential of the community, country and region.

To this end, all future funding should be conditional upon a "sustainability assessment" by the donor and recipient, designed to ensure that the policy, programme or project adds to the potential of the country to create wealth on a sustainable basis.

National and International Institutional Arrangements

The prevailing narrow views and objectives of both agricultural and environmental policy have been reflected in the structure and mandates of public and private institutions concerned with agriculture, especially in most developed countries. Often, the Ministry of Agriculture and/or Forestry has formal responsibility for soil and water conservation, forest protection and watershed management, and some ministries have a proud history behind them. In some countries, beginning in the late 1960s, a new Ministry of Environment has been given responsibility for the conservation of nature, parks and species. In a few countries, the Ministry of Environment is a subagency of the Ministry of Agriculture.

The institutional changes required, nationally and internationally, must begin by recognizing ecological security as a priority goal of agricultural policy in all its manifestations. This goal must become manifest in several ways, most importantly by broadening and reinforcing the mandates of the economic, finance, planning, trade and other central agencies of government, making them individually and collectively responsible for ensuring that their policies do not undermine but rather enhance the ecological basis for food security in the short, medium and long term.

This goal should also be reflected in a strengthening of the agricultural, trade and other relevant mandates of all appropriate international agencies. In turn, the agencies could, for example, strengthen mechanisms for technical co-operation in research among developing countries within regions and among regions by greater support for the existing Technical Cooperation among Developing Countries (TCDC) and Economic Cooperation among Developing Countries (ECDC) mechanisms; and support programmes to establish both national and international data banks. At the same time, donor agencies and international institutions must place higher priority on projects that establish *linkages* between conservation and development in their aid policies and programmes. Natural resource-oriented institutions, such as the International Council for Research on Agroforestry, need to be strengthened and included in the CGIAR networks. Moreover, outstanding research and training institutions dedicated to helping developing countries on strictly non-political and non-commercial lines should be promoted.

Such a strengthening at national and international levels must be real, not symbolic. It should be reflected in the budgets of all national and international agencies. To augment these, it would be necessary to upgrade and marshal professional and other resources needed to reassess existing policies against the criteria of sustainability. To this effect, it would be necessary to develop concerted lending and granting policies and programmes by the donor community with respect to the conservation of the environment. These would include increased assistance to surveying natural resources and making available the resources to enable governments to close lands to production in order to rehabilitate them and to enhance their productivity. Such assistance should be long term in nature, and in the medium term the commitments should extend at least until the year 2000. Additionally, donor countries and international organizations should assist in the strengthening of national research institutions, particularly in Africa.

For their part, developing countries should make greater investment efforts into research and human resource development. We suggest the following as necessary:

1. establish more and expand existing rural agricultural and technical training institutes;
2. with international support, if necessary, develop research in low-cost, small-scale irrigation and drainage schemes by national governments and regional groupings;
3. support research on the integrated application of traditional

97

and emerging technologies and encourage the growth of research programmes developed and undertaken jointly by scientists, technologists and rural families; and

4. support research on the refinement of early warning systems relating to climatic and environmental events.

Regional organizations should be strengthened by both member governments and donor countries, the latter taking care that their support does not distort national priorities. These organizations can also monitor ecological and environmental development and problems on a regional basis.

4. Summary of Major Conclusions and Key Recommendations

We know what needs to be done but do not know how it can be done.

In our Interim Report on the African crisis submitted last year, we indicated the short-term and long-term steps necessary for promoting sustainable food security in countries of the Sahel (Annex 1). Subsequent events have only confirmed our view that a sustainable livelihood security plan for poor farmers and farm labour with particular attention to small producers and women is the only way of achieving food security on a sustainable basis.

We face many challenges that affect the prospects for sustainable agricultural development: social and economic inequities, rapid population growth and youthful demographic structure in developing countries with dire implications for the provision of adequate employment opportunities, increasing resource consumption, environmental degradation and hazards, severe debt burdens, industrial impacts, technological disparities, trade wars, growing defence expenditures, political and institutional disruptions and social unrest, and changing human values and needs.

The world has, fortunately, the necessary technical know-how, financial resources and food reserves to face these problems successfully, both in the short and long term. Numerous national, regional and international conferences have been held on these themes and there is hardly anything new we can say about the linkages between food security, agriculture, forestry and environment that has not been said before, often in a more eloquent and elaborate manner. Why then do we witness, in the midst of this vast pool of existing knowledge on ecological problems and possible solutions, the continuing degradation of the global environment and the almost exponential growth in the number of children, women and men going to bed hungry?

The roots of the problem lie in the nature of decision-making structures at national and international levels. The agricultural economy in virtually all countries is subject to a high degree of governmental intervention. Despite suggestions to the contrary, such intervention is often necessary and may even increase. The real difficulty at the national level is the narrowness of objectives in sectorally fragmented organizations, the disproportionate influence of the rich and the powerful within and outside the nations and the distortion of objectives and policies because of greed and corruption. The urban orientation given to agricultural policies in most developing countries is another impediment to rural livelihood security. The international economic system reinforces these difficulties and adds to them the pressures of price and economic fluctuations which force national governments to take a very short-term view of agricultural development. Ecological considerations can play a more central role in agricultural development only if there is a political will to tackle these weaknesses in decision-making structures at national and international levels.

To reverse current trends in environmental degradation and to promote development without destruction of natural assets, we suggest for the consideration of member countries of the United Nations and the professional community the following Seven Point Action Plan:

1. develop an international code for the sustainable and equitable use of life-support systems;
2. include sustainable livelihood for all in the UN Declaration on Human Rights;
3. initiate a new agricultural system for nutrition security;
4. ensure equality of opportunity for access to technology;
5. organize skills for sustainable livelihood security in every country;
6. reorient international action and assistance so that it is to be consistent with integrated national conservation and sustainable livelihood strategies; and
7. promote political commitment and accountability.

Basic Principles underlying the Action Plan for Food and Environmental Security

To be relevant globally any Action Plan should obviously have a blend of universal and unique features. While the universal features arise from basic human rights and obligations, the unique features should cater to the specific political, cultural, economic and ecological conditions prevailing in each country and, in the case of large countries, within different regions of the country. The Plan, while being capable of responding to varying and changing needs of countries, should not compromise on the following basic principles.

First, sustainable livelihood security for the poor should be the foundation for all development programmes. Mahatma Gandhi of India called such an approach to development the "Antyodaya" model, which in its operational sense implies that priorities in development should be measured by their potential benefit to the poorest sections of the community.

Second, the national and international economic policies which influence agriculture, forestry and related sectors must be reoriented to be based on principles of economic ecology.* The criteria used in the design of specific projects, in the provision of infrastructure, in research and extension, in subsidies and similar incentives must be re-examined and modified to promote the provision of a sustainable livelihood for the poor and to encourage ecologically sound farming practices.

Third, the new orientation means that policies adopted by national and local governments must be consistent with promoting people's participation in the formulation and implementation of development plans and the advancement of a mass-based economic ecology movement. Such an orientation will serve both as a means towards the objective of sustainable development and as an end worth pursuing in its own right.

The pursuit of these basic principles will require a major effort in the restructuring of institutions and the design of development plans.

---

* Economic ecology means development strategies that can help to accelerate economic growth without causing harm to life-support systems.

Ecological considerations are inherently intersectoral in character. Decision-making structures at local, national and international levels will have to be restructured to ensure a higher degree of horizontal co-ordination among activities in different areas such as land-use controls, water management, crop husbandry, horticulture, animal husbandry, forestry, fisheries, rural energy, rural water supply, etc. Institutional restructuring will also be required to provide for more effective people's participation and to improve the access of the poor to land, livestock, water, technology and other resources.

To be meaningful, development plans should be capable of self-replication and thereby of gaining a self-propelling momentum. Too often, externally aided projects collapse when the external inputs are withdrawn. A self-sustaining food and environmental security movement can be launched only with the full participation of the people of every country and by recognizing that enduring nutrition security can be achieved only by safeguarding the basic life-support systems of land, water, flora, fauna and the atmosphere.

While taking the household as an integrated unit in livelihood security programmes, specific attention will have to be given to children and women, since they often constitute the more deprived and vulnerable sections of the household. By paying specific attention to the technological needs and income of women, the total household income and well-being will be enhanced. The reverse procedure of dealing with the household as a homogeneous unit and not paying explicit attention to women and children has often failed to improve women's productivity and income as well as child care and nutrition.

Finally, there is need for an effective monitoring system for keeping a continuous and close watch on the state of the environment as related to sustainable livelihood and food security. At the international level, there has to be an autonomous organization similar to Amnesty International to monitor the impact of human activities on the environment and to issue timely warning on possible harm to sustainable livelihood security arising from human greed and corruption. ''Human heritage'' violations are even more serious because of their adverse impact on the lives of generations yet to be born and hence need as much, if not more, attention as human rights violations.

Action Point 1: An International Code For The Sustainable And Equitable Use of Life-support Systems

The real danger to sustainable food security comes from the greed of the rich and the spread of careless technology. The genuine needs of the poor for fuel and fodder do cause damage in some places. But this damage in its quantitative and qualitative dimensions pales into insignificance when compared to the extensive and often irreversible damage done by commercial forestry and mining operations, careless road construction in undulating terrain, construction of huge dams and reservoirs, highly mechanized agriculture leading to soil erosion, improper irrigation resulting in waterlogging and salinization and multiple industrial pollutants. In order to provide guidelines for the sustainable and equitable use of the basic life-support systems of land, water, flora, fauna and the atmosphere, the development of an appropriate International Code is suggested. An International Code could provide the stimulus for the development and use of an appropriate national code that would contain a checklist of Do's in addition to Dont's with reference to the use of basic agricultural assets.

Conservation should not come to be regarded as a movement for preserving a part of the earth in its pristine purity for the rich to enjoy it. The international and national codes for the sustainable and equitable use of life-support systems should help to foster the concept that conservation is a means of guaranteeing sustainable livelihood security for all human beings at all times. The precise application of the provisions of the code will vary from country to country, since the causes of damage to life-support systems vary widely. For example, certain regions, more particularly developed countries, face problems such as acid rain. However, globally all face stratospheric ozone depletion and the unknown consequences of atmospheric warming due to a higher concentration of carbon dioxide and trace gases in the atmosphere. Land-based pollution of the oceans is becoming increasingly serious. The conservation of gene pools of flora and fauna is essential for successful breeding efforts in economic plants and farm animals in both developing and developed countries. The conservation and wise use of basic national assets

103

such as genetic and water resources are thus shared concerns of people everywhere, and all nations must contribute to this effort. The International and National Codes relating to life-support systems can help to promote positive action based on principles of economic ecology and to monitor the state of the environment at local, national and global levels.

While a code can help to generate awareness of problems and stimulate analysis of local situations in the context of sustainable development, a code itself will be of only academic interest if it is not supported by an implementation mechanism. If the code is to be given meaning and relevance, it has to be implemented and monitored at the level of each village and town. What is needed for this purpose is grassroots-level people's organizations. It is, therefore, suggested that every nation encourage and assist the growth of an ASSOCIATION FOR SUSTAINABLE DEVELOPMENT in every village or cluster of villages. At the country level, such associations could become part of a NATIONAL FEDERATION OF ASSOCIATIONS FOR SUSTAINABLE DEVELOPMENT. At the global level, such National Federations could jointly organize a GLOBAL FEDERATION OF ASSOCIATIONS FOR SUSTAINABLE DEVELOPMENT.

The precise structure of a village-level Association for Sustainable Development will vary from country to country, according to the political organization of local self-government. It is important that the associations remain autonomous in order to maintain their character as people's organizations, but at the same time they should have symbiotic links with existing associations and clubs on one hand and local self-government units on the other. If such associations come into existence, they could become instruments for analysing local problems in environmental management and finding local solutions to local problems.

For example, if the people in a village are short of fuel or fodder, the members of the association can discuss the matter among themselves and propose the most feasible method of meeting such needs on a sustainable basis. Without local-level institutional structures for attending to all links in the awareness-analysis-action chain, the proposed international and national codes for the sustainable and equitable use of life-support systems will remain largely pieces of rhetoric.

There is a need to develop an International Code that will provide the basis for developing detailed national and regional codes for the sustainable and equitable use of the basic life-support systems of land, water, flora, fauna and the atmosphere. The code should provide a new basis for international trade and financial agreements that can safeguard long-term sustainability of food production systems.

Action Point 2 : Sustainable Livelihood Security For The Poor

Once this concept is accepted as the basis of environmental planning, many of the contradictions and internal inconsistencies now occurring in national development plans and international and bilateral assistance programmes may be mitigated. Sustainable livelihood security for the poor as the first priority provides a firm and essential foundation for regional and national long-term development and resource conservation. At present, while preparing forest development and conservation plans, the needs of forest dwellers for livelihoods as well as of the poor for fuel and fodder are rarely kept in view and are almost never the starting point. Social forestry programmes often do not involve the society for whose benefit the programmes are intended. Most agricultural development plans refer to irrigation, seeds, fertilizer, pesticides and implements but seldom start with or include reference to the farming families who are to produce the crops or to pastoralists. Most plans do not consider whether or how women, labourers, marginal or small farm families will gain or lose in livelihood security. Yet, who owns and has rights to trees and tree products, who grows crops or owns livestock and who benefits from resource-based programmes are now more important questions than ever. How much is produced, where it is produced, by whom and with benefits to whom are critical questions for low-income and food-deficit countries, for impoverished regions within countries and for members of poor households. When sustainable livelihood security for the poor is put first and achieved, other regional and national problems diminish or disappear.

Sustainable livelihood development plans should comprise three elements. First, land reform and redistribution: the extension of principles to include livestock, trees and other assets is essential. Through secure ownership of assets, the poor will gain not just livelihoods but personal stakes in conservation. Second, plans should be sensitive to current survival strategies of the poor and seek to strengthen such strategies in a sustainable manner, while supplementing them, as feasible, through including access to rural industries and employment. Third, a balance will be sought, to the extent possible, between the human population of every village or cluster of villages and its natural and other resources to provide the minimum needs of the people for food, water, fuel, fodder and shelter on a sustainable basis. Through ownership, access and security, poor rural people of every village will have incentives to ensure the ecological sustainability of farming systems and other resource use. The conflict between conservation and development will then tend to vanish.

To achieve and support sustainable livelihood security for the poor, it will be essential for governments and international agencies to reorient their priorities and modes of operation. National, Regional, and Local Livelihood Security Plans will vary in detail. They will involve generating purchasing power in rural areas through on-farm and off-farm employment and rural infrastructure development including education and health care. These will create conditions for reduced rural to urban migration and ultimately a stable population. Policies will be required to reverse the current drain of both brains and financial resources from the village to the city. Resource development plans will have to be designed and screened to enhance sustainable livelihoods. Professional training and orientation will have to be turned around to give priority to the poor and to sustainability. For their part, developed countries will have to assess their trade and aid in terms of sustainable-livelihood effects, which are often negative, and ensure that they are made positive. Similarly, international agencies, including the IMF, the World Bank, and regional development banks, must examine and adjust their programmes and projects, the process of structural adjustment and the policy dialogue, in general to ensure positive and not negative livelihood effects in the short as well as long term.

Sustainable livelihood security for all is the only foundation on which enduring food and environmental security can be built. Hence, it is recommended that "sustainable livelihood security for all" be included in the UN Declaration of Human Rights so that appropriate action at the national level can be stimulated.

Action Point 3: Agricultural Systems For Enduring Food Security

Global trends in agricultural research and development indicate that we now have the capability to produce adequate food for existing and future populations. It is also clear that new technologies provide opportunities for increasing production through a vertical growth in productivity and a higher intensity of cropping rather than through a horizontal increase in area (see Figure 4 as an example). This provides the possibility of an ecological foundation to use of land and water. In addition, the untapped production reservoir, even at existing levels of technology, is high in most farming systems of developing countries. Recent advances in biotechnology and other sciences create the confidence that the onward march of agriculture will continue.

Although production prospects are bright, we witness growing rural poverty today as the result of public policies that favour the urban population. At the global level, over 300 million tonnes of grain stocks and over 500 million hungry children, women and men co-exist. International trade patterns in food grains also discriminate against poor nations, since rich countries are able to offer substantial export subsidies and impose import curbs.

There is need for new agricultural systems designed to ensure that at least by 2000 A.D. no child, woman or man goes to bed hungry. Such systems should have the following three major components:

Production: The economies of most developing countries depend largely on land and water-based occupations such as crop husbandry, animal husbandry, forestry and fisheries. Agriculture provides the raw material for many industries. Therefore, if predominantly agricultural countries depend upon

107

imported foodgrains for feeding their population, they will only compound problems of rural unemployment and underemployment. Agricultural development should, hence, be regarded not just as a means of feeding the urban population but as a major instrument of employment and income generation. The first need at the national level, therefore, is a reorientation in the outlook of government and urban populations towards agriculture, which is increasingly becoming a highly skilled and sophisticated profession.

The agricultural technologies developed and propagated should have long-term sustainability as the first principle. Conservation-based agriculture will involve attention to the sustainable management and use of soil, water, flora, fauna and other life-support systems. As emphasized in our Interim Report on Africa, priority attention should be given to the rehabilitation of the ecologically productive base. Often, ecological and agricultural rehabilitation plans can be integrated through agro-forestry, sylvi-horticultural and sylvi-pastoral systems of land management and water conservation.

Developed countries also face many threats to sustained high productivity as a result of soil erosion, pollution of water sources, genetic homogeneity and high consumption of fossil fuel-based inputs. Hence, both developing and developed countries should undertake a review of all aspects of the development and dissemination of technology with a view to ensuring ecological and economic sustainability. In addition, countries with smallholdings should make *smallholder friendliness* a basic feature of agricultural programmes. Often, new technologies may be *scale neutral* with regard to their relevance to small farmers but they may not be *resource neutral*, since inputs and outputs are related. Therefore, public policies should enable all farmers, irrespective of the size of their holdings, other entitlements and risk-taking capacity, to derive economic benefits from new technologies.

While careless technology can cause unmitigated environmental disasters, technologies carefully tailored to specific agro-ecological and socio-economic conditions can help increase food production and at the same time ensure freedom from environmental degradation. Thus, we can keep soil productivity at high levels today through adequate soil-health monitoring and care. We can replenish soil fertility through an integrated nutrient-supply system consisting of organic recycling, green manuring, scientific crop rotation and the use of the minimum essential mineral fertilizers. The leguminous plant *sesbania rostrata* from Senegal is a wonderful nitrogen-producing factory since it fixes atmospheric nitrogen both in the roots and stem. Because of the unusual possibilities now open for raising productivity of both crops and farm animals, we can release marginal lands from annual crops and place them under sylvi-pastoral or sylvi-horticultural or other agro-forestry systems of land and water management. We can minimize or avoid the use of chemical pesticides through integrated systems of pest management.

Similarly, where water is extremely scarce, modern methods based on the delivery of water in closed conduits at high frequency and low volumes directly to the root zone can be modified and simplified to fit the needs of smallholders. Advances in molecular biology provide scope for the development of an integrated genetic conservation strategy ranging from the establishment and protection of biosphere reserves, national parks and other forms of *in situ* conservation, to the creation of DNA libraries, particularly in the case of species threatened with extinction. Above all, the computer and communication revolutions have given us unusual powers for effective monitoring and dissemination of environmental information.

It is necessary, however, to develop new approaches for achieving a proper match between research priorities and strategies and rural realities. In the African context, there is need for strong national research systems capable of carrying out location-specific research, because of the fragility of soils, scarcity of irrigation water, diversity of crops and vagaries of climate. At the international level, institutions that are politically and commercially neutral, such as the Institutes of the Consultative Group on International Agricultural Research (CGIAR), should be strengthened.

In the case of fisheries, we are now in a better position to distinguish between the effects of nature and of human action whenever there is a steep decline in production. The ability to distinguish between the impacts of adverse climatic events that cannot be prevented and those that are the results of political, social and economic policies and/or the products of technology, makes it possible to minimize adverse impacts by matching appropriate solutions to the problems.

In view of the great threat to plant breeding in developing countries as a result of the growing commercialization of plant breeding research in developed countries, supported by patent rights, we must ensure that the world's genetic resources are protected as a public and not as a private resource.

Commerce: National policies on pricing and trade [23] in agricultural commodities must ensure fair returns, particularly to small producers, and promote sustainable patterns of resource use.

International trade patterns should ensure that the concept of "trade rather than aid" as a mechanism of rich nations helping poorer ones becomes a reality. The tendency of industrialized countries to dump surpluses in developing countries, thereby undermining local production, must be curbed to ensure enduring food security.

International trade agreements, tariffs and other economic policies relating to trade in agricultural commodities must deal specifically with the basic task of promoting sustainable resource use.

The policies of all nations must promote the production of agricultural commodities where they are needed and where it is ecologically advantageous to produce them. This will require a major effort at restructuring the global pattern of agricultural production and trade.

Consumption: Food security for the poor need not wait until a country's goal of achieving agricultural self-reliance is achieved. Short-term "Food for Development" programmes based both on locally produced food and on food aid through the World Food Programme and bilateral sources will help to insulate the poor from hunger arising from inadequate purchasing power. Such short-term measures should be coupled with long-term purchasing power improvement programmes to constitute a National Nutrition Security System.

Nutrition Security Programmes should help to provide not only the needed calories and proteins but safe and clean drinking water, and provide for the special needs of children.

Improved post-harvest technology, particularly of perishable commodities, is essential for providing maximum benefit to both the producer and consumer. Aflatoxins (produced by micro-organisms infecting grains) can cause different forms of liver ailments; hence greater attention to drying and storage will be necessary.

Animal husbandry, fisheries and horticulture offer particularly attractive opportunities for rural families in the tropics and sub-tropics to enhance their income directly, as well as through the preparation of value-added products.

The food habits of rich nations and of the rich in poor nations are tending to undergo changes, leading to reduced intake of meat and greater consumption of salad vegetables and fruits. A careful monitoring of shifts in food habits will help developing countries plan for catering to new markets, provided care is taken that this is not done at the expense of their own nutritional requirements.

Unless more on-farm and off-farm employment opportunities are generated in rural areas, the consumption capacity of the ultra-poor (i.e., people without any assets) will remain far below desirable nutritional requirements. A nutrition orientation should, hence, be introduced in all ongoing farming systems' research and development programmes.

Action Point 4: Science and Technology For Sustainable Livelihood Security

A unique opportunity now exists for meeting basic human needs in nutrition and employment on a sustainable basis through a blend of traditional and modern technologies. Biotechnology including tissue culture techniques, technologies for preparing value-added products from biomass, micro-electronics, computer sciences, satellite imagery and communication technology are all aspects of frontier technologies that can enrich rural professions. If steps are not taken to adapt and adopt them for upgrading agriculture, aquaculture and village industries, the poor will be denied the benefits of modern technology for reducing drudgery, increasing productivity and creating diversified opportunities for employment and income. Some aspects of emerging technologies are particularly attractive for rural

111

women, since they can provide flexibility in time and place of work.

The potential opportunities offered by the new technologies can be made effective only if based upon strong and explicit national research priorities. National research priorities in the field of agriculture and rural production should explicitly emphasize the generation of new knowledge and the adaptation of existing knowledge directed specifically to the amelioration and sustainability of the agricultural production in the poor farmer sector. Frontier technologies can be used to develop new, efficient technological solutions for the rural poor and for the reformulation of traditional technologies adapted to local conditions.

Science and Technology

The setting of these priorities will imply major changes in current research priorities in many developing countries by addressing a gap unlikely to be covered by the current directions of global technological change. Specific national science and technology strategies will need to be designed and implemented, including the development of an institutional capacity for management of technological pluralism, that makes best use of the existing human, capital and ecological capacities by blending new, "modern" technologies with traditional technologies.

Ensuring sustainable livelihood for resource-poor farmers presents a special challenge for agricultural research methods and organization. Green Revolution technologies, as applied to date, are better suited to stable, uniform, resource-rich conditions with good water supplies and soils such as alluvial plains and deltas in much of Asia, parts of Latin America and small portions of Africa. Yet it is in the ecologically complex and diverse environments and hinterlands of sub-Saharan Africa, Asia and Latin America, typically with less reliable rainfed conditions, uneven topography and poorer soils, that production and sustainable livelihoods are needed. To serve hinterland and resource-poor farmers, agricultural research has to be more differentiated and sensitive to farmers' conditions and priorities. This needs decentralization and new roles for scientists that will enable resource-poor farmers to articulate their priorities for research, to learn from workshops of farmer innovators, and to allow for joint farmer-scientist R & D and adaptive research on the farm, using research stations for referral, with eventual evaluation by the farmers. The new challenge is the joint development and adaptation of technology by farmers and scientists together.

There is a big gap between knowledge and its utilization because the worlds of the 'giver' and the 'receiver' are apart. Steps must be taken so that knowledge reaches the poor in a form and a language that is related to the experience of the world they live in. This implies an understanding of the context in which knowledge can be used and applied. Analytical knowledge is not enough; it should be transformed into knowledge that is relevant in the context of the multi-dimensional world of poverty. Special attention needs to be paid to making knowledge usable, and for this purpose two-way "laboratory to land" and "land to laboratory" programmes are needed. The rural Associations for Sustainable Development proposed above will be very helpful in making research and extension a joint activity between the rural population and professional scientists and extension workers.

To achieve the above aims, we recommend the following three steps:

Firstly, governments of developing countries should recognize "access to technology" among basic human needs alongside opportunities for literacy, primary health care and clean drinking water now recognized by governments in their priorities for the allocation of public funds. Data banks and information dissemination centres should be set up which will provide the rural poor with information on technologies, weather, market behaviour and opportunities and other relevant economic and scientific information.

Secondly, there is need for national and regional networks of institutions committed to the cause of developing and popularizing integrated applications of traditional and emerging technologies. Such networks should work closely with the local Associations for Sustainable Development.

Thirdly, a low-cost but effective method of skill and knowledge sharing is urgently needed. The present pattern of

113

technical assistance involves a heavy expenditure on pay, perquisites and privileges. The dimensions of the technology upgrading efforts in the rural areas of poor nations are, however, vast; hence, the need for a Rural Resource Corps of Professionals who are willing to share their know-how with the rural poor and work with the villagers in adapting new technologies to suit local conditions. The question of restructuring the UN Volunteers Programme as an effective low-cost mechanism for this purpose deserves consideration.

Equality of opportunity for access to appropriate technology should be regarded by all governments as a basic need of the people. National and international *Rural Resource Corps of Professionals* can be organized for sharing new skills and techniques with rural populations and for collaborating with them in developing location-specific technologies.

Action Point 5: Education For Sustainable Food And Livelihood Security

The task of linking food security, agricultural progress, forestry and conservation within the confines of a sustainable livelihood security strategy is a challenging one. It calls for a systems approach to national resources management and development. It places the well-being of the poor as the foundation of planning. It demands the intensification of efforts in the development and diffusion of technologies relevant to sustainable agricultural growth through appropriate packages of technology, services and government policies. To achieve these goals, a massive effort in education and human capital development is essential. Among the educational tools suggested earlier, the village-level Associations for Sustainable Development and the Rural Resource Corps of Professionals are important.

Illiteracy is still widespread among the rural poor. Hence, along with efforts to promote formal literacy, technical literacy in relation to land use, water and trees should be imparted—a resource literacy through technical skills and work experience. The non-formal education centres, the indigenous puppet plays and other such familiar media and the modern mass media should all be geared to spreading this knowledge, which is essential to promoting harmony in the human environment.

In rural schools, the core of the curriculum must reflect the knowledge a child must acquire for better understanding and management of his/her local resources and for survival. If knowledge is to be relevant, the curriculum must include information about local soils, water and its conservation problems, deforestation and the role of the community and individual intervention in destruction or revival. The teachers must be trained in the knowledge required and the curriculum developed with field needs in mind to link school education with the agriculture of the area. Children should learn the "assets" and "liabilities" aspects of the agriculture sheet of their village/region so that, from early childhood, they become aware of the need to improve their natural assets and minimize the liabilities.

Education of females will help to *motivate* voluntary adoption of the small family norm by:

1. increasing female non-agricultural wage employment opportunities;
2. raising family-income levels through increased direct employment of both husband and wife; and
3. reducing infant mortality through a better understanding of child care and health thereby avoiding the need for many children in order to ensure the survival of a few.

The rapid rise in population in some developing countries coupled with lack of rural development has led to a serious dearth of jobs and purchasing power in many rural areas. This has resulted in large-scale migration of people without any form of assets from villages to towns. Such "environmental refugees" are victims of a breakdown in the balance between human populations and the life-support system of land, water, flora and fauna in their native habitat. Unfortunately, they receive neither attention nor recognition. The generation of an awareness of this problem will be a powerful educational method of arousing consciousness of the need to maintain a symbiotic balance between human populations and their environment. An organization similar to the UNHCR, which deals with political refugees, could help in developing methodologies for measuring and monitoring the influx of environmental refugees into some of the major cities of the world.

We are now in the age of a communications revolution. Many developing nations are investing heavily in communications hardware. But software development, particularly for conveying environmental and livelihood security messages in a simple and effective manner in local languages, does not receive adequate support and attention. There is no need to wait for the spread of formal literacy before unskilled workers become skilled. There are opportunities now for promoting technical literacy in relevant fields through properly designed mass media programmes.

A mass media programme for new skills for sustainable livelihood security needs to be organized in every country. The power of the media for promoting technical literacy and access to inputs and services should be fully utilized, particularly in countries where there is still widespread illiteracy.

Action Point 6: New Orientation To International Action And Assistance

International action and assistance should aim at strengthening national conservation and livelihood security strategies. Hence, new patterns of international assistance are needed that can help promote enduring food security. This will require the development of new approaches to international action. First of all, countries affected by food crises, especially in Africa, should receive international aid to enable them to repair the damage or disruption that has already occurred in the natural ecosystems and prevent the recurrence of such damage. All plans for increasing food production should, therefore, be consistent with an integrated National Conservation and Sustainable Livelihood Strategy. All available national, bilateral and international resources should be pooled and utilized in order to serve that strategy. In this respect, it is important to emphasize the need for financial, commodity and technical assistance to be utilized in such a manner that fosters rather than erodes the spirit of self-reliance. Priority in international assistance should be given to countries adopting such a coherent strategy. Moreover, food aid should not be regarded as an alternative to the development of a national food security plan, but should become a short-term intervention measure to enable affected countries to deal with immediate human distress. It is from this perspective that emergency food aid should be managed in such a way as to increase its efficiency. For instance, emergency aid generally becomes available when calamities (drought and famine) occur. Such assistance ceases once there is an improvement in the weather. It is more efficient if emergency aid is: (a) managed on an internationalized basis; and (b) if it is continued after the crisis until the affected countries regain their ecological balance. All these areas of action require the strengthening of the spirit of multilateral support from developed to developing countries.

To achieve these aims, a new approach to bilateral and multilateral assistance is needed. All agencies should be willing to subordinate their special interests to the overall good of the people of the country they wish to help. National priorities should not get distorted by the pattern of external help offered. On the contrary, all available financial, technical and food and other commodity resources should be utilized in a mutually complementary and reinforcing manner to foster enduring nutrition and livelihood security.

Each country will have to develop a strategy by which all available national, bilateral and multilateral resources of surplus food and other commodities, financial resources and technical expertise can be utilized in a mutually supportive and complementary manner for strengthening national self-reliance.

Action Point 7: Achieving Political Commitment And Accountability

For decades international commissions have produced pious appeals for political will, which in practice means requests that the rich and powerful should act against their own interests. That little has then happened is scarcely cause for surprise. We seek to avoid that trap by securing political commitment and linking it with public accountability by using other methods. The need is so great, and past experience so discouraging, that special efforts seem imperative.

We propose action at local, national and international levels. The five essentials for such action are public political commitment, plans for sustainable livelihood security, local awareness and organization, monitoring and communications, and mechanisms for accountability:

Public political commitment: the main elements are as follows:

1. conferences and workshops to be conceived at international, national and local levels for political leaders to discuss the main thrusts of this report and how they can interpret and implement them;
2. public debates on television and radio inviting political leaders of all countries to state their positions and intentions; these should be repeated at intervals; and
3. inclusion of sustainable livelihood security in political manifestos.

National, subnational and local plans for sustainable livelihood security require the following:

1. local participation plans starting with critical zones such as forests, hinterlands, wastelands, vulnerable catchments and marginal pastoral land;
2. subnational and national plans to follow, as feasible;
3. donor agencies to give priority, as requested, to funding and otherwise supporting well-conceived sustainable livelihood security plans; and
4. plan implementation to be monitored, as elaborated below.

Local awareness and organization requires:

1. public education, voluntary agencies and mass media to be key elements in raising awareness, encouraging active organization and monitoring from below, for articulating and pressing legitimate demands; and
2. national and international networks to be launched linking like-minded groups, particularly Associations for Sustainable Development described under Action Point 1.

Monitoring and communications requires:

1. locally, groups to monitor plans and progress;
2. nationally, organizations to collate and publish data, as for example the "Citizens' State of the Environment Report" of the Centre for Science and Environment in India;
3. internationally, a suitable independent body to: monitor sustainable livelihoods and the environment, obtain and give wide dissemination to satellite data, act as watchdog on unethical and corrupt practices and constitute a livelihood and environmental equivalent of Amnesty International. If we value an organization such as Amnesty International because of its role in arousing the conscience of humanity by drawing attention to gross violations of human rights and dignity, a similar organization is urgently needed to help generate widespread awareness of violations to human (natural) heritage and life-support systems through greed and/or corruption; and
4. international and national visits for mutual learning and support to be arranged by an organization such as the proposed Global Federation of Associations for Sustainable Development.

Accountability should be secured through:

1. television interviews and discussions at regular intervals;
2. public hearings where projects threaten livelihoods;
3. free circulation of information by radio and television, both nationally and internationally;
4. monitoring by groups as above; and
5. annual meetings, preferably on a regional basis, at which governments report on their performance over the previous year.

These measures are synergistic. On their own, none may have great effect. Taken together, with resolution, we believe they can be the crucial last link for sustainable development with adequate and secure livelihoods for all.

Achieving political commitment and accountability is basic

119

to success. Fostering political sensitivity and accountability requires the generation of new data and free public access to data. Mass media should become important channels for getting political leaders to make public commitments to the cause of sustainable environmental and livelihood security. Accountability should be strengthened through an independent international body to monitor and disseminate information and act as a watchdog in support of independent monitoring at local and national levels of the damage to the natural heritage and life-support systems caused by human greed.

The above Seven-Point Action Plan has been developed in a manner that will be helpful for examination and action by both governmental and non-governmental agencies. For example, the Ministries or Departments of Government that will be most concerned with initiating action on the different components of the Action Plan are:

1. *Code for Life-Support Systems*
   Department of Environment
2. *Livelihood Security for the Poor*
   Department of Rural Development
3. *Agricultural Systems*
   Departments of Agriculture and Commerce
4. *Science and Technology*
   Departments of Science and Technology
5. *Education*
   Department of Education
6. *Resource Utilization*
   Department of Finance and Foreign Affairs
7. *Political Commitment*
   Political Parties and Leadership

The Action Plan to be effective should be considered and implemented in an integrated manner. Obviously, the relevance of the specific suggestions contained in the Action Plan will vary widely depending upon the socio-economic and socio-political systems prevailing in each country.

Footnotes

1/ World Hunger Project: Ending Hunger: An Idea whose time has come (New York, 1985).

2/ Food and Agricultural Organization, *1984 Production Yearbook,* Vol. 38 (Rome, 1985).

3/ Alan Gear, ed: *The Organic Food Guide* (Essex, 1983).

4/ F.A.O.: *Agriculture: Toward 2000* (Rome, 1981).

5/ P. Justman: "Towards the Year 2000: The Latin American Dilemma", in *Mazingira* (March, 1984) pp 35-39.

6/ World Food Council: "Food Policy Adjustments in Latin America and the Caribbean in support of Food Security and Development". *Ministerial Consultation on food policies and strategies in Latin America and the Caribbean* (Buenos Aires, 1-3 April 1986).

7/ Taken from CASAR, 1986: "Programas Alimentarios Nacionales en América Latina y el Caribe: una respuesta a la crisis económica". Ibid.

8/ F.A.O.: Various *Food Outlooks* ; Economic Commission for Europe (ECE): Various *Agricultural Reviews* for Europe.

9/ F.A.O.: Passim.

10/ F.A.O.: *Agriculture: Toward 2000.*

11/ H. Tabatabai: "Food Crisis and Development Policies in sub-Saharan Africa" (Working paper. International Labour Office, Geneva, 1985).

12/ F.A.O.: *Agriculture: Toward 2000.*

13/ See: Georghiou, G.P. and R. Mellon: "Pesticide Resistance in Time and Space" in *Pest Resistance to Pesticides* (New York, 1983), pp 1-46.

14/ Alan Gear, ed: *op. cit.*

15/ *Ibid.*

16/ Dana Silk: "Urban Agriculture" (paper prepared for the World Commission on Environment and Development (WCED), 1985. Mimeo).

17/ R. Repetto: "Creating Incentives for Sustainable Forest Development" (prepared for WCED, 1986. Mimeo).

18/ World Bank: *Desertification in the Sahelian and Sudanian Zones in West Africa* (Washington, 1984).

19/ P. Shamulanga: Interview with S. Muntemba. Zambia (1985).

20/ See: J. Bandyopadhyay: Rehabilitation of Upland Watersheds (paper written for WCED, 1985. Mimeo).

21/ Based on I. Szabolcs: "Agrarian Change" (prepared for WCED, 1985. Mimeo).

22/ International Union for the Conservation of Nature: *World Conservation Strategy* (Gland, 1980).

23/ Refer also to section on Reorienting Agricultural Policies in this Report (pp.103).

Bibliography

Commissioned papers

Banage, W.B: "Policies for the Maintenance of Biological Diversity"

Bandyopadhyay, J : "Rehabilitation of Upland Watersheds"

Chidumayo, E.N : "Fuelwood and Social Forestry"

Dourojeanni, M.J : "Humid Tropical Forests"

Ecole National d'Economie Appliqur e, Senegal : "Assessment of the Plan of Action to Combat Desertification"

Fundacin Natura: "Women and Food Production in Latin America"

* Repetto, R : "Money Down a Rathole: Pesticide Subsidies in the Third World and Public Policy"

——————————: "Creating Incentives for Sustainable Forest Development"

Silk, D : "Urban Agriculture"

Szabolcs, I : "Agrarian Change"

* World Resources' Institute: *The World's Tropical Forests, A Call for Accelerated Action*

Non-Commissioned papers

Ayensu, E.S : "The African Crisis : An Open Challenge". Mimeo, 1985.

Bandyopadhyay, J. et al : *India's Environment Crises and Responses*. Dehra Dun, 1985.

Brown, L. and E. Wolf : *Reversing Africa's Decline*. Worldwatch Paper 65. Washington, 1985.

Centre for Women's Development Studies : "Role and Participation of Women in the Chipko Movement in the Uttarkherd Region in Uttar Pradesh, India'', in S. Muntemba, ed., *Women and Rural Development,* Geneva, 1985. pp 173-193.

* The Commission contributed to the cost of the World Resources' Institute's studies.

Carnell, P. : *Alternatives to Factory Farming.* An economic appraisal. London, 1983.

Chambers R. : ''The Crisis of Africa's Rural Poor: perceptions and priorities''. Discussion paper (IDS, Sussex) 1985.

Chambers R. and B. Ghildyal: ''Agricultural Research for Resource-Poor Farmers: the Farmer-First-and-Last Model''. Discussion Paper (IDS, Sussex) 1985.

Conway, G.R.: ''Agricultural Ecology and Farming Systems Research'' (London, 1985. Mimeo).

Consumer Association of Penang : *Pesticide : Problems, Legislation and Consumer Action in the Third World:* the Malaysian Experience.

Culik, M. et al : *The Kutztown Farm Report,* Rodale Research Centre, 1983. dale Research Center, 1983.

Daniel, P. et al : ''Towards a strategy for the Rural Poor in sub-Saharan Africa''. Discussion Paper (IDS, Sussex) 1984.

Dichter, D : *Mobilizing Youth and Students for Reforestation and Land Reclamation.* Geneva, 1978.

Eicher, C.K : ''Facing up to Africa's Food Crisis'', *Foreign Affairs.* (Fall, 1982) pp 151-173.

Fresco, L : ''Food Security and Women : Implications for Agricultural Research''. Mimeo, 1985.

Garcia, R : *Food Systems and Society* : a conceptual and methodological challenge. Geneva, 1984.

Gear, A. ed : *The Organic Food Guide.* Henry Doubleday Research Association. Essex, 1983.

Ghai, D. and S. Lawrence: *Food Policy and Equity in sub-Saharan Africa.* ILO Working Paper. Geneva, 1985.

Grainger, A: *Desertification,* How People Make Deserts, How People Can Stop and Why They Don't; London, 1984 reprint.

ICRAF : *Criteria for Reappraisal and Redesign: Intra-household and between household aspects of FSRE in Three Kenyan Agroforestry Projects.* Nairobi, 1985.

International Development Research Centre: *Symposium on*

Drought in Africa. Manuscript Report. Ottawa, 1985.

International Union for the Conservation of Nature: *World Conservation Strategy*. Gland, 1980.

McNamara, R : *The Challenge for sub-Saharan Africa*. Washington, 1985.

Muntemba, M.S : "Women as Food Producers and Suppliers in the Twentieth Century", *Development Dialogue 1982*: 1-2, pp 29-50.

————————: "The Structural Causes of Hunger". Mimeo. 1985.

Myers, N : "The Hamburger Connection": How Central America's Forests Become North America's Hamburgers, *Ambio* 10 (1), pp 3-8. 1981.

————————: "Deforestation in the Tropics : Who Gains, Who Loses?" *Studies in Third World Societies 13*, 1982. pp 1-24.

Palmer, I : "The Impact of Agricultural Development Schemes on Women's Roles in Food Supply". Mimeo. 1985.

Peek, P : *Rural Poverty in Central America: Dimensions, Causes and Policy Alternatives*. ILO Working Paper. Geneva, 1984.

————————: *Agrarian Reform and Poverty Alleviation: the Recent Experience in Nicaragua*. ILO Working Paper. Geneva, 1984.

Sen, G : "Changing International Perspectives Towards Women and Food—an appraisal". Mimeo. 1985.

Shiva V. and J. Bandyopadhyay : *Ecological Audit of Eucalyptus Cultivation*. Dehra Dun, 1985.

Swaminathan, M.S : *Agricultural Progress—Key to Third World Prosperity*. London, 1983.

————————: *Agricultural Research and the Challenge of Conservation, Commerce and Consumption*. New Delhi. 1986.

Tabatabai, H : *Food Crisis and Development Policies in sub-Saharan Africa*. ILO, Working Paper. Geneva. 1985.

Timberlake, L : *Africa in Crisis*: the causes, the areas of environmental bankruptcy. London, 1985.

United Nations : *Conference on Desertification*. 1977.

UNEP : *General Assessment of Progress in the Implementation of the Plan of Action to Combat Desertification 1978-1984*. 1984.

UNFAO : Agriculture: Toward 2000. Rome. 1981.

——————————: Various *Production Yearbooks.*

——————————: Various *Food Outlooks.*

——————————: *Food Aid for Development.* Rome. 1985.

——————————: *Land, Food and People.* Rome. 1984.

——————————: *World Food Report.* Rome.

——————————: *Approaches to World Food Security.* Rome.

——————————: *Commodity Review and Outlooks 1984-1985.* Rome. 1985.

Weir, D. and M. Schapiro : *Circle of Poison.* Pesticides and People in a Hungry World. San Francisco, 1981.

World Bank : *Poverty and Hunger* : Issues and Options for Food Security in Developing Countries. Washington, 1986.

World Bank: Desertification in the Sahelian and Sudanian Zones in West Africa (Washington, 1984. Restricted Distribution).

World Resources Institute : *World Resources 1986.* An Assessment of the Resource Base that Supports the Global Economy. Virginia, 1986.

——————————: *Getting Tough* public policy and the management of pesticide resistance. Washington, 1984.

Annex

Interim Recommendations to WCED on the Food and Ecological Crisis in Africa

Introduction

At our first meeting, held in Geneva on 12-13 May 1985, we gave detailed consideration to the short- and long-term implications of the African Food Crisis and decided to make the following interim recommendations to WCED for consideration at its next meeting in June 1985. We hope that these recommendations will be implemented as soon as possible by the Governments/bilateral/UN agencies concerned.

Basic Guidelines

Protecting the livelihood of the poor, ensuring livelihood to the destitute and very poor, providing basic goods and services in rural areas and optimizing the benefits of existing educational and developmental infrastructure are the most urgent tasks. Helping the poor to earn their daily bread has to be the primary strategy for promoting economically and ecologically sustainable development. In addition, steps to develop food security systems will have to be based on the following basic facts:

1. More than enough food is already produced in the world to provide a balanced diet for all its inhabitants;
2. People with purchasing power seldom go hungry;
3. Small and subsistence farmers will not produce more than what they need for themselves, unless they are assured cash

and/or goods acceptable in exchange for the surplus;

4. Food imports by predominantly agricultural countries will have the same impact as importing unemployment, since imports will lead to keeping local farmers at low levels of productivity and employment;

5. Youth and the poor constitute the two genuine majorities in most developing countries. Hence, any development plan for sustainable development based on sound principles of ecology and economics which fails to involve them both as participants and beneficiaries is unlikely to yield the expected benefits.

Recommendations

The following four sets of recommendations are offered for immediate consideration and implementation:

Food Security

1. Food aid and emergency relief.
   We commend the on-going efforts in providing the needed food aid and other forms of assistance to the drought stricken countries. Such assistance has helped to save many lives and has provided the breathing spell necessary for the initiation of agricultural and ecological rehabilitation efforts. We expect that continued efforts will be made to achieve a well-integrated programme of relief operations, capable of reaching everyone in need of help.

2. Incentives to small producers: Programme for the supply of cash and basic goods.
   Remunerative prices coupled with the supply of basic goods such as clothing, salt, soap, blankets, cooking oil, matches, sugar, batteries, paraffin, paper, pencils will help to stimulate small farmers to produce and earn more. We therefore recommend that out of the amount available for emergency relief, a certain proportion be reserved for purchasing at remunerative prices surplus produce from small producers. Both cash and the basic goods farm families need can be given in exchange for locally produced agricultural com-

modities. Thefood grains thus procured may be utilized within that country for operation of "Food for Work" programmes for assetless agricultural labour families.

The basic goods to be supplied may include not only consumer and household goods but also farm inputs such as seeds, fertilizers, etc. If such a small producers' incentive plan is intelligently prepared and imaginatively implemented, there will be an immediate upward swing in agricultural production and productivity in many African countries.

A self-replicating and propelling growth pattern can be hastened by using external aid to end the prolonged need for such aid.

Livelihood Security

The Livelihood Security plan will have to cover poor farmers and farm labour with particular attention to women and small producers. In years of acute distress, assets such as land, livestock and trees are usually sold by the poor who thus become assetless. The challenge lies in preventing such distress sales. There is need for a multi-pronged strategy for Livelihood Security consisting of:

1. enabling poorer households to own assets such as goats, sheep, poultry, cattle and trees;
2. introducing an Employment Guarantee Scheme for unskilled labour such as the one operating in the Maharashtra State of India, which is a chronically drought prone State; and
3. developing and popularising technologies which can help to generate more on-farm and off-farm employment and income.

Agricultural and Ecological Rehabilitation

Even as human life-saving operations are in progress, no time should be lost in initiating steps for strengthening the ecological infrastructure essential for sustained agricultural advance. A National Ecological and Agricultural Rehabilitation Plan should be developed for this purpose in each country. Such a plan should consist of a portfolio of well-defined tasks. Once the tasks to be implemented are carefully defined, steps should be taken to identify the most appropriate agency (Government, non-governmental, bilateral, UN or other multilateral agencies, etc.) for implementing each specific task.

Such a Task Adoption approach will help the country to derive the maximum advantage from the specific expertise and competence of different national and international agencies. The aim should be the integration of external and internal inputs in such a manner that the benefits from all available institutional, technical and financial resources are optimised. The proliferation of programmes and agencies should be avoided. An integrated national Eco-development and Agricultural Rehabilitation Board with representation to all the task adopting agencies should be set up.

International Eco-development Corps for Africa
We recommend the immediate organization of an Eco-development Corps of young professionals for helping to find effective solutions to location specific problems. There is urgent need for developing location specific technologies and approaches for agricultural rehabilitation and eco-development in Sahelian countries. Generalised prescriptions and programmes should be avoided, since they do more harm than good. Present patterns of technical assistance are very expensive and cannot be replicated on a scale necessary for generating a critical mass of meaningful efforts. The following will be some of the principal characteristics of the International Eco-development Corps for Africa:

1. The Corps should consist of young professionals, preferably in the age group 20 to 30, drawn from the African countries concerned and from all over the world. They will thus be joint teams of nationals and foreigners. The persons selected for serving in the Corps should have a combination of desirable professional skills and personal qualities, particularly humility and compassion.
2. The African Eco-development Corps should constitute a special component of the UN Volunteers Programme but will be administered under the guidance and direction of an International Technical Advisory Committee (TAC). TAC will consist of eminent scientists, technologists, educationists, social scientists and development administrators known both

for their knowledge of African problems and their concern for harnessing science for the welfare of the poor.

3. The members of this African Eco-development Corps should serve on a modest honorarium and should look upon the opportunity given to them as an opportunity for learning and service.

Conclusion

We believe that through concerted efforts in promoting ecologically and economically sound food production plans coupled with steps to ensure livelihood security to the poor and remunerative prices to the small producers, the present crisis can be converted into an opportunity for rapid advances in agricultural progress and agrarian prosperity. By tapping the imagination, know-how and commitment of young professionals both from developed and developing countries in the challenging task of making hunger a problem of the past in drought-ravaged Africa, we will not only help Africa but will provide a unique opportunity for working and learning together.